Torah Story
Workbook

Torah Story
Workbook

GUIDED

EXERCISES

in the

PENTATEUCH

GARY EDWARD

SCHNITTJER

 ZONDERVAN
ACADEMIC

ZONDERVAN ACADEMIC

Torah Story Workbook
Copyright © 2023 by Gary Edward Schnittjer

All maps: Copyright © 2023 Gary Edward Schnittjer. All rights reserved.

All tables, charts, and figures: Copyright © 2023 Gary Edward Schnittjer. All rights reserved.

Requests for information should be addressed to:
Zondervan, *3900 Sparks Dr. SE, Grand Rapids, Michigan 49546*

Zondervan titles may be purchased in bulk for educational, business, fundraising, or sales promotional use. For information, please email SpecialMarkets@Zondervan.com.

ISBN 978-0-310-11283-9 (softcover)
ISBN 978-0-310-11284-6 (ebook)

Cover design: Gearbox Studio
Cover photos: © Tanner Mardis; Taylor Wilcox / Unsplash
Interior design: Kait Lamphere

Printed in the United States of America

23 24 25 26 27 28 29 30 31 32 33 34 35 36 37 38 /VPI/ 20 19 18 17 16 15 14 13 12 11 10 9 8 7 6 5 4 3 2 1

CONTENTS

A NOTE ON BIBLICAL TRANSLATION

This book uses the New International Version (NIV) for Scripture quotations unless stated otherwise. The NIV has been modified with permission by using Yahweh for "the LORD," Torah or torah as an English loanword for "Law" or "law," and Messiah for "Christ." Translations marked as "lit." (literal) are mine.

A NOTE TO STUDENTS

The activities in this *Workbook* are designed to help process the *Torah Story* textbook and the scriptural contexts associated with each chapter as well as to take some next steps.

Please have a copy of the Scriptures open and *Torah Story* on hand to make the most of the activities. The first activity of each *Workbook* chapter reviews key elements of the chapter in the textbook. The last activity in each *Workbook* chapter offers you an opportunity to work out selected implications. The other activities in each chapter work through a range of elements with an eye to the scriptural context and the textbook.

You are encouraged to take your time. Worthwhile outcomes including connections and implications often require effort.

A NOTE TO PROFESSORS

The activities in this *Workbook* aim at student outcomes. They can help students prepare for class sessions and other course assignments.

The activities in this *Workbook* are interactive and hands-on. The *Workbook* questions do **not** reproduce the questions in the textbook. Here is a comparative chart reproduced from the textbook regarding the purposes of the available learning activities.

Interactive Workshops at end of main Chapters of *Torah Story*	Activities in *Workbook*	Selected resources available at no cost in TextbookPlus
• **Key Terms** are suitable as a basis for short quizzes or minor in class review • **Challenge Questions** primarily focus on the discussion in the respective chapter of the textbook—suitable for class discussions, online discussion forums, and individual study assignments • **Advanced Questions** lead students to apply the discussion of the respective chapter of the textbook to case studies in the Torah itself—suitable for class discussions, online discussion forums, and individual study assignments • **Research Project Ideas**	• **Activity 1** focuses on reviewing leading elements of the respective textbook chapter (without significant overlap of Challenge Questions and Advanced Questions in the textbook itself) • **Activities 2 and following** feature case studies focusing on geography, biblical connections, difficult passages of Torah, and the like • **Making It Our Own Activity** (final activity in each chapter) provides opportunities for students to work through select implications of their studies	• **Visual Aids** • **Quizzes** • **Exams** • **American Stories and the Torah Story** are activities based on old movies or Bible movies—ideally suited for class discussions or as individual study assignments • **Quizzes** on *Torah Story Videos* • **Answer Key** to the *Workbook*

As noted in the chart, for an *Answer Key to the Workbook* for professors at no cost, please see TextbookPlus at ZondervanAcademic.com or reach out to your Zondervan Academic representative.

The pages in the *Workbook* are not perforated so students can keep their work all in one place. To submit homework students can capture images of assigned activities and put them in a Microsoft Word file or a slideshow file such as PowerPoint to submit on the class page—or students can print the file for professors who prefer submission of hardcopies.

For a few additional comments just for professors please see "A Note to Professors on the *Answer Key to the Workbook*."

Paul Venning

ACTIVITY 1: *Getting Started (Chapter Opening and Starting Points)*

1. The Torah story is the beginning of the _____.

2. Where in the Bible does the gospel begin?
   a) Genesis 1:1
   b) Matthew 1:1
   c) John 3:16
   d) Romans 1:1

3. Who did Moses write about? _____

4. What does Torah with a capital "T" refer to?
   a) the Ten Commandments
   b) the first set of stone tablets the Moses broke
   c) Genesis, Exodus, Leviticus, Numbers, and Deuteronomy
   d) the laws God gave Moses on Mount Sinai

5. What does torah with a lowercase "t" refer to?
   a) nothing, Torah should always be capitalized
   b) instruction
   c) the other laws God gave to Moses besides the Ten Commandments
   d) legalism

6. What term best describes the genre or literary form of the Torah?
   a) narrative
   b) law
   c) legal minutia
   d) biography

7. How many books of the Torah tell a story? _____

1

ACTIVITY 2: *The Documentary Hypothesis (Sidebar 1-A)*

1. What do the letters stand for in the so-called Documentary Hypothesis—J? _____, E? _____, D? _____, P? _____

2. Why did the proponents of the Documentary Hypothesis date the Priestly (P) parts of the Torah as later than other parts?

3. Liberal modern Protestants valued older as better and they were "_____" the oldest parts of the Pentateuch, created in their own _____—stripped of ritual, legal, and miraculous elements.

ACTIVITY 3: *What Biblical Narratives Do (Biblical Narrative as Theological Interpretation)*

1. A biblical narrative provides a _____-shaped framework that explains who characters are within the _____ and according to the plot.

2. What is the function of a narrative's ending?
 a) its destiny
 b) to bring joy
 c) to surprise
 d) to allow people to move to the next thing

3. The two endings of the story that begin in the Torah—the new beginning for Israel on the bank of the Jordan River and the _____ of Messiah—are the _____ that explain the meaning of the story.

4. What is the relationship between event and narrative?
 a) narratives are not related to events
 b) biblical narratives do not interpret events but present factual accounts
 c) events and biblical narratives are one and the same
 d) narratives are interpretations of events

5. John told his story the way he did to _____ his readers of the identity of Messiah that they would _____ in him.

6. What makes biblical narratives theological?

    a) biblical narrative is God's story

    b) pastors and theologians add theology to the narratives

    c) only faithful Christian readers can use narratives theologically

    d) all Christians, even when living in sin, add theology to the narratives

7. What do biblical narrators expect?

    a) biblical narrators do not expect anything; they are simply scribes taking dictation from God

    b) biblical narrators expect readers to see that their stories are just the facts with no "spin"

    c) biblical narrators intend for their stories to shape readers' lives

    d) biblical narrators expect faithful Christian leaders to add good theology to their factual stories

8. Biblical narrative is not simply the most _____ book. Biblical narrative is the story within which _____ lives.

ACTIVITY 4: *How Biblical Narratives Work (Responsible Interpretation of Biblical Narrative)*

Matching

1. ___ The goal of responsible interpretation	**A**	includes symbolic significance
2. ___ First reading	**B**	reading in light of the whole
3. ___ Second reading	**C**	reading forward
4. ___ Narrative space	**D**	may include flashbacks or previews
5. ___ Narrative sequence	**E**	biblical narrative itself

Matching

6. ___ cause to effect and effect to cause	**A**	parallel repeated sequencing of similar elements
7. ___ climax	**B**	repeated elements at opening and closing
8. ___ comparison	**C**	suppressing an expected element to emphasize it
9. ___ contrast	**D**	linking elements in a consequential relationship
10. ___ extended echo effect	**E**	the point to and from which a narrative ascends and descends
11. ___ ellipsis	**F**	elements which anticipate what will come later
12. ___ foreshadowing	**G**	juxtaposing dissimilar elements
13. ___ framing	**H**	juxtaposing similar elements
14. ___ generalization	**I**	moving from specific to broad

Matching

15. ___ interchange	**A**	element which simultaneously points back and forward
16. ___ janus	**B**	second half repeats similar elements in reverse order
17. ___ leading word	**C**	element which signals a change of direction in the narration
18. ___ mirror imaging (chiastic structure)	**D**	alteration of elements to heighten irony, comparison, or the like
19. ___ particularization	**E**	using rhyming, oral effects, puns, and the like to create ironies or other kinds of emphasis
20. ___ proportion	**F**	emphasis by quantitative attention
21. ___ turning point	**G**	running themes using identical terminology or associated word clusters
22. ___ typological patterns	**H**	moving from general to specific
23. ___ wordplays	**I**	expectational similarities of persons, events, or other elements

ACTIVITY 5: *Making It Our Own* (*Biblical Narrative as Theological Interpretation*)

1. Why is it important to recognize that biblical narratives do more than repeat the facts of historical events?

2. How does biblical narrative offer *direction* to readers?

2 INTRODUCING THE TORAH

ACTIVITY 1: *Understanding the Chapter (An Overview, A Reading)*

1. Elements of Torah that point toward its unity and coherence include _____ connections between each book and interconnected imagery such as the Song of Moses speaking of a mother eagle "_____" over its young in a way that echoes creational and redemption themes.

2. What is the problem with the traditional translation of torah as "law"?

3. Why is the traditional title "the Law" not a good fit for the Torah of Moses?
   a) Moses grew up in Egypt where they did not have courts and did not need laws
   b) the Torah is a story
   c) the term "law" could lead to legalism
   d) it could create confusion between the Ten Commandments and the Pentateuch

4. What is the Torah's story?

5. How does the expectation for a prophet like Moses cause the future to look like the past?

ACTIVITY 2: *Matching the Book (An Overview, A Reading)*

Fill in the following blanks with single letters G (Genesis), E (Exodus), L (Leviticus), N (Numbers), or D (Deuteronomy).

1. _____ The traditional name for this book reflects its contents as instructions for priests

2. _____ The rebellion of humankind

3. _____ The traditional name for this book refers to the two censuses

4. _____ God's glory descends to the tabernacle

5. _____ The traditional name for this book refers to the liberation from slavery

6. _____ This book includes the great commandment to love God

7. _____ The promise of land, seed, and blessing to the Hebrew ancestors

8. _____ Two generations of rebels in the wilderness

9. _____ The traditional name for this book comes from "a copy of the teaching"

10. _____ God calls out to Moses from the tent of meeting

11. _____ The people wandering in the wilderness

12. _____ The burning bush

13. _____ Instructions to live with the holiness of God

14. _____ The traditional name for this book means "origins"

15. _____ Three discourses from the other side of the Jordan River

16. _____ God speaks from the mountain

ACTIVITY 3: *Making It Our Own (Another Look)*

1. In what ways do Moses and Paul agree on the function of Torah?

2. What does Paul tell Timothy is a good function of the Torah?

3 MACROVIEW OF GENESIS

SSG Randy Welchel

ACTIVITY 1: *Understanding the Chapter (A Reading)*

1. The book of Genesis serves as a _____ within which the rest of the Bible and the entire human story fits between the _____ days and the _____ days.

2. Genesis is comprised of two sections, namely, the beginning of _____ (Gen 1–11) and the beginning of the _____ _____ (12–50).

3. What does the extended echo effect in Genesis 1–11 tell readers about God and the scriptural narrative?

4. What are important similarities between the stories of Abraham, Jacob, and the sons of Jacob?

5. The three major elements of the Abrahamic promise are _____, _____, and _____.

6. What do the "accidents" in Genesis suggest about the way God works?

ACTIVITY 2: *The Hebrew Ancestors (A Reading)*

1. How long did Abraham have to wait before his offspring or "seed" arrived?

    a) 9 months

    b) 7 years

    c) 12 years

    d) 25 years

2. Which of the Hebrew ancestors does not get a separate set of stories?

    a) Abraham

    b) Isaac

    c) Jacob

3. Which of the Hebrew ancestors gets a new name because he wrestled with humans and God?

    a) Abraham

    b) Isaac

    c) Jacob

4. Which of Jacob's sons gets the birthright (double portion)?

    a) Reuben

    b) Judah

    c) Joseph

    d) Benjamin

5. Which of Jacob's sons gets the blessing (rulership)?

    a) Reuben

    b) Judah

    c) Joseph

    d) Benjamin

ACTIVITY 3: *Narrative Framework of Genesis (A Reading)*

1. Place the following on the correct dotted line: • Beginning of chosen family; • Beginning of humankind

2. Place the following in historical sequence on the lines in the left-hand box: • Adam; • Beginning; • Noah; • Shem, Ham, Japheth

3. Place the following in the correct places on the lines to the right-hand side in the three boxes or under the two arrows: • Abraham; • Esau; •Ishmael; • Jacob; • Sons of Jacob

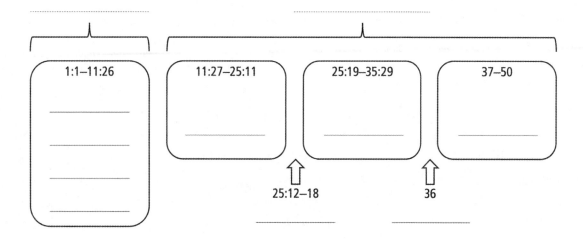

ACTIVITY 4: *Making Connections across Scripture (Another Look)*

1. How does the opening of Genesis serve as the beginning relative to the ending of the Torah?

2. How does the opening of Genesis serve as the beginning relative to the ending of the Primary Narrative?

ACTIVITY 5: *Making It Our Own*

1. What do the recurring patterns of the Genesis story tell us about the human problem?

2. How do the recurring patterns of the Genesis story help strengthen one's trust in God?

4 THE BEGINNING
(Genesis 1:1–2:4a)

ACTIVITY 1: *Understanding the Chapter (A Reading)*

1. "In the beginning" is important because it simultaneously serves as the introduction to Genesis, to the _____, to the Hebrew Scriptures, and to the entire _____.

2. What are options for how the author knew of the account of creation?

3. Besides the *ruah* over the waters in Genesis 1:2, the term reappears in Genesis and Exodus to evoke similar imagery in the cases of the "_____" of the day (Gen 3:8); to clear the flood water when God _____ Noah (8:1); and to make a way of salvation through the _____ (Exod 14).

4. What is death?

5. The fourth creating day is "_____-centered" because the celestial lights are placed in the heavens to give _____ to the earth dwellers and to mark the times and seasons of the earth dwellers. Even to describe the cosmic lights in terms of "_____" and "_____" measures time with reference to the experience of the earth dwellers.

6. How do the two great commands—love God and love others—portray the implications of humans created in the image of God?

7. In what ways does the seventh day function with respect to the six creating days?

ACTIVITY 2: *Ancient Near Eastern and Biblical Cosmologies (Sidebars)*

1. What are examples of concrete imagery used in Genesis to depict the cosmos?

2. The most notable similarity between Enuma Elish and the creation narrative in Genesis is when Marduk split _____ into two parts, using one half to make the _____ above.

3. What is a difference between the creation narrative in Genesis and creation myths of Israel's rivals?

ACTIVITY 3: *Narrative Framework of Genesis 1 (A Reading)*

1. Place the following on the correct dotted line: • Filling; • Forming

2. Place the following on the correct lines within the boxes: • birds and fish; • celestial lights; • heavens and waters; • land animals and humans; • light and dark; • waters and land

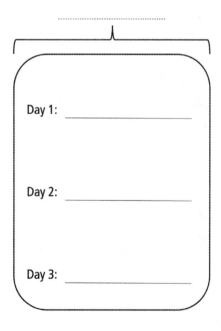
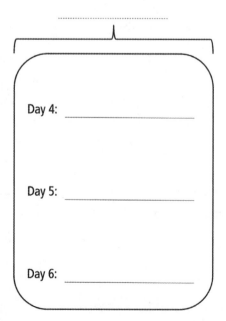

ACTIVITY 4: *A Close Reading of Genesis 1*

First-person discourse means to speak of oneself (I, me, we, us), second person to directly address another (you), and third person to talk about another (she, he, it, they, them, their).

1. <u>Underline</u> all of the third-person phrases "according to its(their) kind(s)" in the narration of creation days 3, 5, and 6 (see below).

   How many are there? _____

2. Use <u>wavy underlining</u> to mark cases of first-person phrases referring to God's own likeness, singular or plural, in day 6 (see below).

   How many are there? _____

3. Use <u>broken underlining</u> to mark cases of third person phrases of in God's own likeness or image, singular or plural in day 6 (see below).

   How many are there? _____

> [**Day 3**] ⁹And God said, "Let the water under the sky be gathered to one place, and let dry ground appear." And it was so. ¹⁰God called the dry ground "land," and the gathered waters he called "seas." And God saw that it was good. ¹¹Then God said, "Let the land produce vegetation: seed-bearing plants and trees on the land that bear fruit with seed in it, according to their various kinds." And it was so. ¹²The land produced vegetation: plants bearing seed according to their kinds and trees bearing fruit with seed in it according to their kinds. And God saw that it was good. ¹³And there was evening, and there was morning—the third day . . .
>
> [**Day 5**] ²⁰And God said, "Let the water teem with living creatures, and let birds fly above the earth across the vault of the sky." ²¹So God created the great creatures of the sea and every living thing with which the water teems and that moves about in it, according to their kinds, and every winged bird according to its kind. And God saw that it was good. ²²God blessed them and said, "Be fruitful and increase in number and fill the water in the seas, and let the birds increase on the earth." ²³And there was evening, and there was morning—the fifth day.
>
> [**Day 6**] ²⁴And God said, "Let the land produce living creatures according to their kinds: the livestock, the creatures that move along the ground, and the wild animals, each according to its kind." And it was so. ²⁵God made the wild animals according to their kinds, the livestock according to their kinds, and all the creatures that move along the ground according to their kinds. And God saw that it was good.
>
> ²⁶Then God said, "Let us make humankind in our image, in our likeness, so that they may rule over the fish in the sea and the birds in the sky, over the livestock and all the wild animals, and over all the creatures that move along the ground." ²⁷So God created humankind in his own image, in the image of God he created them; male and female he created them. ²⁸God blessed them and said to them, "Be fruitful and increase in number, fill the earth and subdue it. Rule over the fish in the sea and the birds in the sky and over every living creature that moves on the ground." (Gen 1:9–13, 20–28; vv. 26–27 lit.)

4. What are the implications of the shift from repeated third-person "according to their kinds" to first-person plural "according to our kind"?

ACTIVITY 5: *Making It Our Own*

1. 1. What is a better approach than when readers try to use the scriptures to answer their own questions?

2. What is the significance of Jesus the Messiah as being the very image of God in human form in Philippians 2:6–7?

3. What are the implications of people in the likeness of God in James 3:9–10?

5 THE GARDEN AND THE EXILE
(Genesis 2:4b–4:26)

Jon Cooper

ACTIVITY 1: *Understanding the Chapter (A Reading)*

1. What did the highest and most responsible beings in God's creation decide to do early on?

2. God brings before the man all of the animals to _____ before God created the woman to show the man his need for _____.

3. What is the social orientation of being known as "woman" versus as "Eve" in Genesis 2–3?

4. The positive sense of the name "_____" points to the hope of humans that comes through her offspring as "_____ of the living," and yet part of her curse is suffering in _____ (Gen 3:16, 20).

5. What are two inanimate elements that get literarily "personified" in Genesis 4?

6. How many times is the word "brother" used in Genesis 4:1–12? _____ This repetition strengthens the perversity of the murder of _____.

7. What is the sense of the numbers "seven" and "seventy-seven" in the poem of Lamech—the seventh generation from Adam and Eve through Cain—to his wives (Gen 4:23–24)?

ACTIVITY 2: *Competing Interpretations of the First Prohibition (A Reading)*

1. Using the text of Genesis 3:1–6 below, underline the verbal repetitions of the prohibition against eating from the tree of the knowledge of good and evil (Gen 2:17) in the speeches of the serpent (3:1, 4–5) and the woman (3:2–3).

2. Use wavy underlining to mark the place(s) that the serpent distorts the prohibition.

3. Use broken underlining to mark the places in the woman's allusion to the prohibition against eating from the tree that she expands upon the prohibition itself.

> [16]And Yahweh God commanded the man, "You are free to eat from any tree in the garden; [17]but you must not eat from the tree of the knowledge of good and evil, for on the day you eat from it you will certainly die." (Gen 2:16–17; v. 17 lit.)

> [1]Now the serpent was more crafty than any of the wild animals Yahweh God had made. He said to the woman, "Did God really say, 'You must not eat from any tree in the garden'?" [2]The woman said to the serpent, "We may eat fruit from the trees in the garden, [3]but God did say, 'You must not eat fruit from the tree that is in the middle of the garden, and you must not touch it, or you will die.'" [4]"You will not certainly die," the serpent said to the woman. [5]"For God knows that when you eat from it your eyes will be opened, and you will be like God, knowing good and evil." [6]When the woman saw that the fruit of the tree was good for food and pleasing to the eye, and also desirable for gaining wisdom, she took some and ate it. She also gave some to her husband, who was with her, and he ate it. (3:1–6)

4. Why is it unclear if the woman added to the prohibition or if the man added to the prohibition?

5. What is ironic about the serpent's explanation of the effects of disobeying the prohibition?

ACTIVITY 3: *The Meaning of Death in Genesis 2–3 (A Reading)*

Yahweh told humans they would certainly die "on the day" they ate from the fruit (Gen 2:17 lit.). But they did not drop dead. So it is necessary to investigate what happened to humans when they rebelled to understand *what it means to die*.

Fill in the following chart by identifying what changed on the day humans rebelled against the command of God using language from these verses: • Gen 3:7, 9–11; • Gen 3:12, 16; • Gen 3:17–18; • Gen 3:22–24.

What changed in . . .	
. . . the relationship between humans and God?	hiding from Yahweh (3:8)
1. . . . the relationship between humans and self?	
2. . . . the relationship between humans and creation?	
3. . . . the relationship between humans and other humans?	
4. . . . the relationship between humans and life?	

ACTIVITY 4: *Identifying Key People (A Reading; Genesis 2–4)*

Fill in the empty cells.

	Scripture reference?	Relation to Adam?	Best known for?
1. Eve	3:1–6, 13, 16, 20		
2.	4:1–16	eldest son	
3.			keeper of sheep
4. Lamech		seventh great-grandson through Cain	
5. Seth	4:25		

ACTIVITY 5: *Making It Our Own (Another Look)*

1. What can be learned about the new life from John 10:10, 11:25–26, and 17:3?

2. What may be deduced by comparing the effects of eating from the tree of life and believing in Messiah according to John's Gospel?

6 THE FLOOD AND THE NATIONS
(Genesis 5–11)

Ted Rabbitts/CC BY 2.0

ACTIVITY 1: *Understanding the Chapter (A Reading)*

1. The major structural connectors from the primeval setting in Genesis 1–11 to the Hebrew ancestors in Genesis 12–50 are the two ten-generation genealogies. The first goes from Adam to _____ (Gen 5) and the second from Noah to _____ (11:10–26).

2. The judgments by flood and by giving languages to the tower builders are both _____ in scope.

3. The genealogy of death in Genesis 5 ends with an identical phrase, namely, "_____" for every person except for _____ and Noah.

4. Two people in the genealogy of death in Genesis are said to "walk with God," namely, _____ and _____.

5. The sons of God took in marriage the _____ of humans and produced the _____ (Gen 6:4).

6. Noah took _____ of every kind of animal and _____ of ritually clean animals onto the ark to preserve a remnant.

7. The curse of _____ was interpreted in a sinful way to produce false doctrines to justify brutal racial slavery.

8. While the builders all worked together to make a tower up to the _____, Yahweh needed to _____ _____ to see the tower.

19

ACTIVITY 2: *Timeline of the Flood (A Reading)*

1. Fill in the blanks with the correct number of days in the upper part of the timeline as well as identifying the month in the blanks below the timeline.

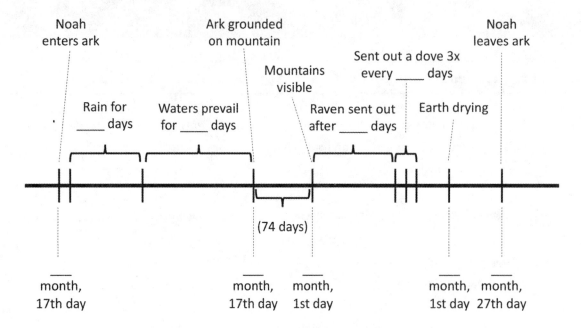

2. How does the perspective of the narrative change when "God remembered Noah"?

ACTIVITY 3: *The Flood in Genesis and Gilgamesh (Sidebar)*

Fill in the blank with either Gen for Genesis, EG for Epic of Gilgamesh, or both.

1. Humankind is too noisy. _____
2. Humankind is too sinful. _____
3. Divine decision to destroy all humankind. _____
4. Protagonist is warned to build a boat. _____
5. Protagonist, his family, and animals are saved in the boat/ark. _____
6. Rain for six days and nights. _____
7. Rain for forty days and nights. _____
8. Boat lands on a mountain. _____
9. Birds are released to test the levels of the water. _____

10. A dove does not return.   _____

11. Protagonist makes a sacrifice.   _____

12. Promise not to destroy by flood again is remembered through rainbow.   _____

13. Flood is remembered through necklace of jewels.   _____

14. What is the most important difference between the flood narratives of Genesis and the Epic of Gilgamesh?

ACTIVITY 4: *The Sin of Ham (A Reading)*

Several "sin stories" in the Torah seem to be designed with intentional ambiguity, including the sin of Cain, the sin of Ham, the sin of Aaron's sons, and the sins of Moses and Aaron. The purpose of this activity is to investigate possible interpretations of the sin of Ham based on clues within the scriptural text.

1. What evidence in Genesis 9:20–27 is used to support a view that Ham either lusted after or shamed Noah?
   a) Ham drew a picture of Noah on wood using a burnt stick and showed his brothers
   b) Ham sang a song with perverse lyrics about Noah
   c) Shem and Japhet covered Noah without looking at his nakedness
   d) Shem and Japhet told Ham not to look in Noah's tent

2. What evidence in Genesis 9:20–27 and Leviticus 18:7–8 (compare NIV and ESV, use BibleGateway.com if needed) is used to support a view that Ham had sexual relations with Noah?
   a) the euphemism of uncover the nakedness can refer to sexual relations with a person
   b) the language of uncover the nakedness creates mirror imaging (chiastic structure) with the curse of Canaan
   c) both Genesis and Leviticus include a curse against Ham's same sex assault of Noah
   d) Genesis contains the narrative and Leviticus the curse against Ham for his sin

3. What evidence in Genesis 9:20–27 and Leviticus 18:7–8 (compare NIV and ESV, use BibleGateway.com if needed) is used to support a view that Ham had sexual relations with Mrs. Noah?
   a) Shem told Japhet he saw Ham rape Mrs. Noah
   b) Shem told Japhet he saw Ham have consensual relations with Mrs. Noah
   c) Shem told Noah he saw Ham have consensual relations with Mrs. Noah
   d) the euphemism of uncover the nakedness can refer to sexual relations with a person's spouse

4. What are possible reasons that the biblical narrator designed selected sin stories in Torah with intentional ambiguity (see discussion of 6:1–4 in the textbook Chapter 6, and for more detail, see discussion of the sin of Moses in Chapter 22)?

ACTIVITY 5: *Making It Our Own (Another Look)*

1. What did Isaiah have in mind by using the phrase "like the days of Noah" to encourage his constituents?

2. How did Messiah use the phrase "like the days of Noah" in his Mount of Olives discourse to warn his followers?

7 THE ABRAHAM NARRATIVES
(Genesis 12:1–25:18)

A.D. Riddle/BiblePlaces.com

ACTIVITY 1: *Understanding the Chapter (A Reading, Bible)*

1. What are the three parts of the Abrahamic promise?

2. Narrative time is not constant. The closer the reader gets to the birth of the offspring, the _____ time passes (cf. Figure 1-B in Chapter 1).

3. What element of the covenantal ritual between Abram and God in the vision of Genesis 15 suggests that it was a permanent covenant?
   a) The stars of the heavens would take forever to count
   b) The sand of the sea would take forever to count
   c) Abram did not pass through the cut animals
   d) The sun going down symbolized forever in ancient cultures

4. Which character's drunkenness can be compared to Lot's drunkenness in Genesis 19?

5. What three people groups are associated with the first two episodes of drunkenness in Genesis? _____, _____, _____

6. What important issue is established by God's rescue of Sarah from Abimelech?

7. The call of Abraham in Genesis 12:1 includes three things Abraham needed to leave behind: "Go forth from your _____, your _____, and your _____ _____." The test of Abraham in Genesis 22:1 emphasizes three aspects of his promised offspring he needed to sacrifice: "Take your _____, your _____ _____, the one you _____, and go forth."

8. The end of the Abraham narratives echo in a broad sense the call of Abraham in Genesis 12:1–3. Genesis 23 focuses on securing _____ to bury Sarah, Genesis 24 on securing a _____ for his son of promise Isaac, and Genesis 25:1–8 on sending away Abraham's many other children from his second wife _____ to retain the full blessing of inheritance on Isaac.

ACTIVITY 2: *"Accidental" Pregnancies (A Reading)*

Important parts of scriptural narratives pivot on who knows what. Sometimes readers are more well informed than major players in the narration itself.

1. <u>Underline</u> the daughters' secret plans that readers know about even though Lot does not.

2. Use <u>broken underlining</u> to mark the daughters' illicit actions that readers know about even though Lot does not.

3. Use <u>wavy underlining</u> to mark what the narrator tells readers that Lot does not know.

> [30] Lot and his two daughters left Zoar and settled in the mountains, for he was afraid to stay in Zoar. He and his two daughters lived in a cave. [31] One day the older daughter said to the younger, "Our father is old, and there is no man around here to give us children—as is the custom all over the earth. [32] Let's get our father to drink wine and then sleep with him and preserve our family line through our father." [33] That night they got their father to drink wine, and the older daughter went in and slept with him. He was not aware of it when she lay down or when she got up. [34] The next day the older daughter said to the younger, "Last night I slept with my father. Let's get him to drink wine again tonight, and you go in and sleep with him so we can preserve our family line through our father." [35] So they got their father to drink wine that night also, and the younger daughter went in and slept with him. Again he was not aware of it when she lay down or when she got up. [36] So both of Lot's daughters became pregnant by their father. [37] The older daughter had a son, and she named him Moab; he is the father of the Moabites of today. [38] The younger daughter also had a son, and she named him Ben-Ammi; he is the father of the Ammonites of today. (Gen 19:30–38)

4. How had Lot treated his daughters when they still lived in Sodom earlier in Genesis 19 that might help explain why they did not trust their father to be looking out for their best interests?

5. Why do you think it is important to the narrator to inform readers of things that Lot did not know?

ACTIVITY 3: *Test of Abraham (A Reading)*

Fill in the blank with either "F" for foreground, meaning the narration makes it explicit to readers, or "B" for background, meaning the narrator lets readers wonder about it. Look carefully at the details of Genesis 22 to decide.

1. God was only testing Abraham ____

2. What Abraham was thinking about for three days as he went to the mountain ____

3. Abraham made preparations for a sacrifice ____

4. Whether Abraham informed Sarah of his plans ____

5. Abraham misinformed Isaac of his plans for what he intended to sacrifice ____

Fill in the blank with either "before," meaning the reader knew the outcome before the characters in the narrative acted, or "after," meaning the reader did not know until the characters in the narrative acted.

6. God did not really want Abraham to sacrifice his son _____

7. When Abraham said God would provide, he spoke better than he knew _____

8. The Messenger of Yahweh planned to stop Abraham from sacrificing his son _____

9. The ram was caught in a thicket _____

10. The obedience of Abraham would provide opportunity to reaffirm the promises _____

ACTIVITY 4: *Abrahamic Promise (A Reading; Genesis 12–22)*

God reveals more about his promises to Abraham as they go along. Put a checkmark in the contexts that reveal details about the elements of the promise. Genesis 13:14–18 is completed as an example.

	Gen 12:1–3	13:14–18	15:16–21	17:1–16	22:16–18
land		✓			
descendants		✓			
blessing/ relationship		–			

ACTIVITY 5: *Geography Associated with Abraham (A Reading; Genesis 12–25)*

For help with geography activities, the best option is a biblical atlas from a library. In addition, many Bibles have maps near the back, or you can use the maps in *Torah Story*.

1. On the map below:
   o Place a dot on the location of the city where Abraham was born and write the name next to it (Gen 11:28).
   o Do the same for the location where he left the household of his father (11:31–12:1).
   o Draw a circle around the region where Abraham initially settled in the land of promise and write the name in the region (12:9).
   o Write the name of the country where Abraham sought refuge during a famine (12:10).
   o Now draw arrows between these four locations to represent the early travels of Abraham (not through the desert).

   Note: "Yahweh said to Abram after Lot had parted from him, 'Look around from where you are, to the north and south, to the east and west. All the land that you see I will give to you and your offspring forever'" (Gen 13:14–15).

2. Fill in the blanks.

King _____ who lived in Gerar took Sarah into his harem.

The place Abraham almost sacrificed his son: _____ _____

According to 2 Chronicles 3:1 the _____ of Yahweh was built here in the city of _____

The cities of the plain including Sodom and Gomorrah as well as Zoar are located near this body of water: _____ _____

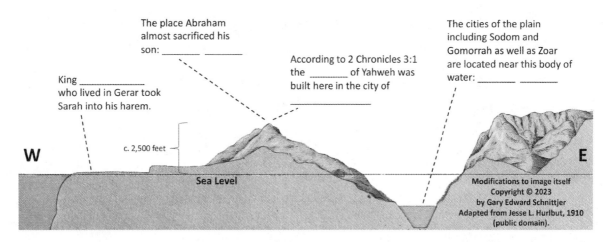

W

c. 2,500 feet

Sea Level

E

Modifications to image itself
Copyright © 2023
by Gary Edward Schnittjer
Adapted from Jesse L. Hurlbut, 1910
(public domain).

3. Fill in the blanks.

The Cave of _____ that Abraham purchased to bury Sarah is in this city: _____

The mountain on which Abraham found a ram caught in a thicket: _____

Joshua 24:1 says Joshua spoke to Israel from _____ which is between Mounts Gerizim and Ebal

Plains of the _____ _____ chosen by Lot (Gen 13:11)

Mount _____ is called Sirion by the Sidonians (Deut 3:9)

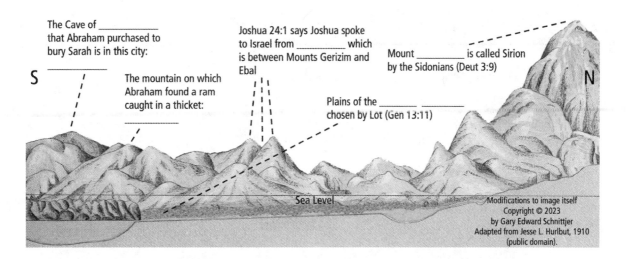

S

N

Sea Level

Modifications to image itself
Copyright © 2023
by Gary Edward Schnittjer
Adapted from Jesse L. Hurlbut, 1910
(public domain).

4. Fill in the blanks.

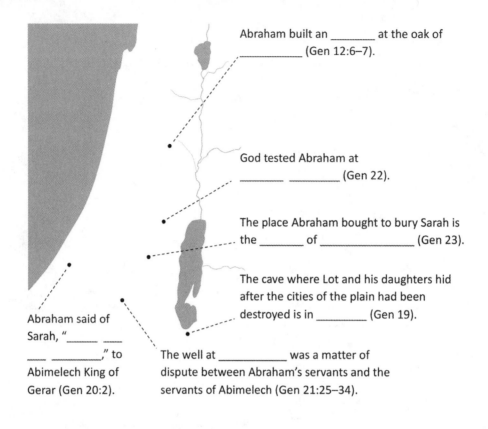

Abraham built an _____ at the oak of _____ (Gen 12:6–7).

God tested Abraham at _____ _____ (Gen 22).

The place Abraham bought to bury Sarah is the _____ of _____ (Gen 23).

The cave where Lot and his daughters hid after the cities of the plain had been destroyed is _____ (Gen 19).

Abraham said of Sarah, "_____ ___ ___ _____," to Abimelech King of Gerar (Gen 20:2).

The well of _____ was a matter of dispute between Abraham's servants and the servants of Abimelech (Gen 21:25–34).

ACTIVITY 6: *Making It Our Own (Genesis 15:6)*

The very same events in Scripture sometimes teach more.

1. Compare Genesis 15:6 and Nehemiah 9:7–8, 32–33 to fill in each blank with the correct person's name. Abraham is the subject of "believe" and _____ is the object in Genesis 15:6. Yahweh is the subject of the verbs and _____ is the object in Nehemiah 9:6–7. _____ is reckoned as righteous in Genesis 15:6 and the Levitical intercessors proclaim _____ as righteous in Nehemiah 9:32–33.

2. Why do the Levitical intercessors shift the focus of Abraham's faith to God (Neh 9:8, 32)?

3. According to Romans 4:9–12, what is one of the purposes of Abraham's faith being reckoned as righteousness before he was circumcised?

4. What is the definition of Abraham's faith in Romans 4:21?

5. Who are among the beneficiaries of the narrative interpretation: "it was credited to him as righteousness" according to Romans 4:22–25?

8 THE JACOB NARRATIVES
(Genesis 25:19–36:43)

Isaiah and Abby Cramer

ACTIVITY 1: *Understanding the Chapter (A Reading)*

1. Jacob seems to embody at one time both the human problem and the _____ _____.

2. The people of Edom are named after the _____ _____ for which Esau sold his birthright.

3. What are the two panels of Jacob's life that the reader sees in his thirteen years with Laban after Jacob married two sisters?

4. Isaac and Rebekah's story with Abimelech is a virtual copy of whose story?

5. Which two sons of Jacob caused trouble for him by deceiving and killing the men of Shechem?

6. Near what city did Jacob lose Rachel?
- a) Jebus
- b) Shechem
- c) Bethlehem
- d) Horeb
- e) Beersheba

7. _____ heard about _____ committing incest with Rachel's former slave Bilhah after Rachel died.

8. What detail in Genesis 36 demonstrates that some of the persons in the list of Edom's kings date to at least the time of Saul and David?

ACTIVITY 2: *Baby Wars (A Reading)*

All of the male children of Jacob's various wives, except Judah, are named after the baby contest between Leah and Rachel. Fill out the chart below—a few are completed for you.

	mother's name	reference in Gen	significance of name to the baby competition between Leah and Rachel
Reuben	Leah	29:32	Leah thought bearing a son would cause Jacob to love her
1. Simeon			
2. Levi			
Judah	Leah	29:35	Leah praised Yahweh for Judah without regard to the baby contest
3. Dan			
4. Naphtali			
5. Gad			
6. Asher			
7. Issachar			
8. Zebulun			

	mother's name	reference in Gen	significance of name to the baby competition between Leah and Rachel
9. Joseph			
10. Ben-Oni (see NIV text note at BibleGateway.com)		35:18	

11. Why might Joseph's name be the most tragic of those in the dysfunctional family of Jacob and his competing wives?

12. The name Judah in Hebrew—*yehudah*—sounds like the Hebrew word *yadah* "to praise." How does his mother make a wordplay on his name in Genesis 29:35 and how does his father make a wordplay on his name in Genesis 49:8?

ACTIVITY 3: *Geography Associated with Jacob (A Reading)*

For help with geography activities, the best option is a biblical atlas from a library. In addition, many Bibles have maps near the back, or you can use the maps in *Torah Story*.

1. Place the name of the locations near the appropriate dots on the map: • Where Jacob lived before he left home—Genesis 28:10; • Where Jacob had a dream of a ladder reaching into the heavens—Genesis 28:11–22; • Where Jacob first kissed Rachel—Genesis 29:4–14.

2. Draw arrows between these locations to indicate Jacob's travels.

3. How long did Jacob work for Laban for brides (Gen 29:15–30)? _____ years

4. For flocks (31:36–42)? _____ years

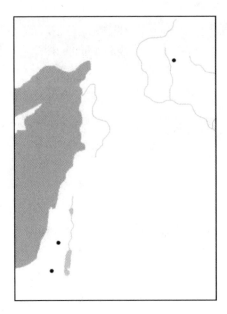

5. On the map below, draw an arrow from the north to the place near where Jacob wrestled in the night (Gen 32:22–32).

6. Draw a dotted line with an arrow in the direction that Jacob told Esau he would go (Gen 33:12–16; cf. 32:3).

7. Draw an arrow in the direction Jacob actually traveled (Gen 33:17).

8. Draw an arrow to indicate where Jacob settled during this time of his life (Gen 33:18).

9. What are the names of Jacob's three children who had serious trouble in this city (Gen 34)? _____, _____, and _____

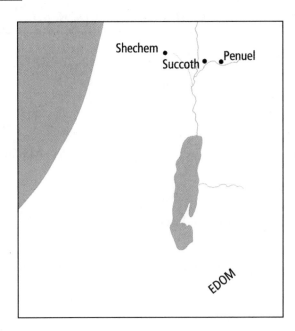

ACTIVITY 4: *A Close Reading of Two Revelations (Genesis 28 and 35)*

1. Underline the parallel language in Genesis 28:18–19 and the counterpart in Genesis 35:14–15 in the text below.

2. Use broken underlining to mark God's promises to Jacob in Genesis 28:11–17 and 35:9–13.

> ¹¹When he reached a certain place, he stopped for the night because the sun had set. Taking one of the stones there, he put it under his head and lay down to sleep. ¹²He had a dream in which he saw a stairway resting on the earth, with its top reaching to heaven, and the angels of God were ascending and descending on it. ¹³There above it stood Yahweh, and he said: "I am Yahweh, the God of your father Abraham and the God of Isaac. I will give you and your descendants the land on which you are lying. ¹⁴Your descendants will be like the dust of the earth, and you will spread out to the west and to the east, to the north and to the south. All peoples on earth will be blessed through you and your offspring. ¹⁵I am with you and will watch over you wherever you go, and I will bring you back to this land. I will not leave you until I have done what I have promised you." ¹⁶When Jacob awoke from his sleep, he thought, "Surely Yahweh is in this place, and I was not aware of it." ¹⁷He was afraid and said, "How awesome is this place! This is none other than the house of God; this is the gate of heaven." ¹⁸Early the next morning Jacob took the stone he had placed under his head and set it up as a pillar and poured oil on top of it. ¹⁹He called that place Bethel, though the city used to be called Luz. (Gen 28:11–19)

> ⁹After Jacob returned from Paddan Aram, God appeared to him again and blessed him. ¹⁰God said to him, "Your name is Jacob, but you will no longer be called Jacob; your name will be Israel." So he named him Israel. ¹¹And God said to him, "I am God Almighty; be fruitful and increase in number. A nation and a community of nations will come from you, and kings will be among your descendants. ¹²The land I gave to Abraham and Isaac I also give to you, and I will give this land to your descendants after you." ¹³Then God went up from him at the place where he had talked with him. ¹⁴Jacob set up a stone pillar at the place where God had talked with him, and he poured out a drink offering on it; he also poured oil on it. ¹⁵Jacob called the place where God had talked with him Bethel. (35:9–15)

3. In the two divine pronouncements to Jacob in Genesis 28 and 35, what does God promise to give to Jacob's descendants?

4. What does God promise to Jacob's descendants and the families of the earth in Genesis 28:13–15 that he does not repeat in Genesis 35:11–12?
   a) All peoples will be blessed through you
   b) The land is given to you and your descendants
   c) Your descendants will include kings
   d) Your descendants will never serve as slaves in Egypt

5. What does God add to his promises to Jacob in Genesis 35:11–12 that he had not mentioned in Genesis 28:13–15?

    a) All peoples will be blessed through you

    b) The land is given to you and your descendants

    c) Your descendants will include kings

    d) Your descendants will never be taken captive

ACTIVITY 5: *Making It Our Own (A Reading)*

1. What can we learn from Jacob praying God's word back to Yahweh in Genesis 32:9–12?

2. What phrase in his prayer of Genesis 32:9–32 is a sign of Jacob's attitude toward Yahweh? What phrase is a sign of his attitude toward his brother? What underlying attitude do these phrases represent? How does Jacob's attitude toward Yahweh and Esau in this time of anxiety provide a model for readers?

9 THE SONS OF JACOB NARRATIVES
(Genesis 37:1–47:26)

Gary Edward Schnittjer

ACTIVITY 1: *Understanding the Chapter (A Reading)*

1. The _____ is a double portion of the inheritance. The _____ vests leadership upon a descendant.

2. According to 1 Chronicles 5:1–2 Joseph gets the _____ and Judah gets the _____ of rulership.

3. The pattern of younger over older in Genesis includes _____ over Cain, _____ over Ishmael, and _____ over Esau.

4. The pattern of temporarily infertile matriarchs includes Sarah, _____, and _____.

5. In Genesis 34 and 35 the pattern of treachery among the brothers includes the three oldest: _____, _____, and _____. What did they do?

6. It is the idea of _____, supported by the brothers, to sell Joseph to merchants, who also dealt in human trafficking, on their way to Egypt.

7. If the patterns of younger over older, the temporarily infertile matriarch, and the treachery of the oldest ten _____ are put together, as well as Joseph sold on the Egyptian slave market, the only one left to inherit birthright and blessing at the end of Genesis 37 is _____.

8. Because Judah does not know his sons' wickedness, who does he assume is to blame for their deaths?
   a) The midwives
   b) Tamar
   c) Himself for selling Joseph
   d) Shelah

9. When _____ showed Judah his own seal and cord he signified his own self-_____, something like repentance, by declaring, "She is righteous, not I."

10. _____ lost another cloak; this one in the hands of Mrs. _____ when he refused to have relations with her.

11. Who unsuccessfully tries to convince Jacob to allow Benjamin to go to Egypt?
    a) Judah
    b) Benjamin
    c) Issachar
    d) Reuben

12. The high point of the story is when _____ offers himself in place of his brother _____.

ACTIVITY 2: *Matching People and Actions (Genesis 37–47)*

1. ___ Incarcerated for one year in an Egyptian prison
2. ___ Imprisoned for attempted rape
3. ___ "Accidentally" had relations with his daughter-in-law
4. ___ Insists he will never stop mourning for his dead son
5. ___ Fails to save Joseph
6. ___ Fails to use his two sons as collateral in an attempt to take Benjamin to Egypt to get food
7. ___ Yahweh put two of his sons to death for their wicked acts
8. ___ Dreams of stellar lights bowing before him
9. ___ Delivers Benjamin from the lord of Egypt
10. ___ Decodes dreams of prisoners and the king of Egypt
11. ___ Accused of stealing the sorcery goblet of the lord of Egypt
12. ___ Served as an Egyptian slave
13. ___ Offered himself as an Egyptian slave to save his youngest brother
14. ___ Became angry with his sons for failing to deceive

A   Reuben
B   Simeon
C   Judah
D   Joseph
E   Benjamin
F   Jacob

ACTIVITY 3: *Hebrew Ancestral Family Tree (Genesis 12–50)*

Place the names on the correct blanks on the family tree: • Abraham, • Asher, • Ben-ammi, • Benjamin, • Dan, • Dinah, • Ephraim, • Esau, • Gad, • Isaac, • Issachar, • Jacob, • Joseph, • Judah, • Laban, • Leah, • Levi, • Lot, • Manasseh, • Moab, • Naphtali, • Perez, • Rachel, • Rebekah, • Reuben, • Simeon, • Terah, and • Zebulun.

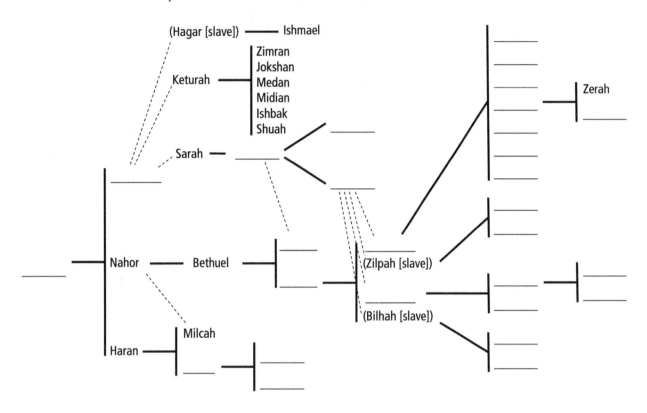

ACTIVITY 4: *Steps in the Transformation of Judah (A Reading, Gen 37–46)*

1. List in proper narrative sequence by filling in blanks with 1st, 2nd, 3rd, and 4th.

   _____ Judah's two oldest sons die when successively married to Tamar.

   _____ Judah marries a Canaanite woman.

   _____ Judah devises a plan to get rid of Joseph by means of human trafficking.

   _____ Judah's wife dies.

2. List in proper narrative sequence by filling in blanks with 5th, 6th, 7th, and 8th.

   _____ Judah "accidentally" gets his daughter-in-law Tamar pregnant.

   _____ Judah travels to Timnah to shear his sheep.

   _____ Judah seeks to burn Tamar to death because she became pregnant by cheating on her betrothed husband Shelah.

   _____ Judah unknowingly gives his seal and cord as collateral (as a "pledge") to Tamar who is disguised as a prostitute.

3. List in proper narrative sequence by filling in blanks with 9th, 10th, 11th, and 12th.

_____ Judah makes an agreement with his father that Judah himself shall be collateral—a "pledge"—to guarantee that he will return Benjamin.

_____ Judah offers himself as a slave to the lord of Egypt in place of his brother Benjamin because he is collateral (a "pledge") in an agreement to protect him.

_____ Judah confesses that Tamar is "righteous, not I" when she reveals he is the man who got her pregnant.

_____ Judah leads the family of Israel on their sojourn to Egypt.

4. How do readers know that Judah's confession of self-humiliation that Tamar is "righteous, not I" serves as a turning point in his life?

5. What terms connect Judah's personal turning point and the high point in the story when he offers himself in place of his brother?

ACTIVITY 5: *Making It Our Own (Another Look)*

1. How does Psalm 51 reveal David's character as the person Yahweh had chosen to be king? How does this differ from and resemble the self-humiliation of Judah?

2. In what respect is the expected king Genesis-shaped?

3. What aspects of the example of Messiah in Philippians 2:5–11 stand as turning points to his exaltation?

10 THE LAST DAYS
(Genesis 47:27–50:26)

ACTIVITY 1: *Understanding the Chapter (A Reading)*

1. What is the significance to all of Scripture that Genesis begins by looking back to the "beginning days" (Gen 1) and ends by looking ahead to the "last days" (49:1)?

2. Jacob gives a double portion (birthright) to Joseph by blessing _____ and _____ who will be ancestors of tribes just like the brothers of Joseph.

3. Jacob speaks negative last words to _____ because he committed incestuous adultery with or raped his stepmother _____.

4. Jacob speaks negative last words to _____ and _____ because they massacred the men of _____.

5. Why did the brothers say that Jacob had instructed Joseph to forgive them after he had already done so?
- a) They thought Joseph had lied about his dreams
- b) They were afraid that he would take his revenge now that their father was dead
- c) They remembered Joseph had pretended not to know them when they had come to Egypt for food
- d) Joseph sent Simeon back to prison again after Jacob died

6. Why might the narrator not describe Jacob as "old" and "full of years" as he did with Abraham and Isaac—compare Genesis 25:8, 35:29, and 49:33?

7. Besides Jacob, who else requested that his body be taken out of Egypt to be buried?

   a) Judah

   b) pharaoh

   c) Joseph

   d) Benjamin

ACTIVITY 2: *Hebrew Poetry (Sidebar)*

1. Why does the older view of parallel lines of Hebrew poetry saying the same thing twice distort how Hebrew poetry works?

2. Compare the details in Exodus 14:26–28 and 15:1, 4, 21. The poetic imagery of _____ Egyptian warriors into the sea poetically closes to the larger conflict between Yahweh and pharaoh in Exodus that began with the Egyptians _____ Hebrew infant males into the _____.

3. Use the translation of Genesis 49:9 (lit.) in sidebar of *Torah Story* ("Reading Hebrew Poetry") for this question and the next. How do lines y and z illustrate the newer view of Hebrew poetry as dynamic with each line developing the previous line?

4. What does it mean to say that lines y and z of Genesis 49:9 (lit.) in sidebar of *Torah Story* ("Reading Hebrew Poetry") use mirror imaging or chiastic structure (the student may wish to review mirror imaging in *Torah Story*, chapter 1)?

5. How does the elevated language of Hebrew poetry strengthen the expectations often presented in the poems of the Torah?

ACTIVITY 3: *Evil Intentions and Good Outcomes (A Reading, Genesis 50:19–20)*

1. Read Genesis 37:21–22 and 37:26–27. What details lead some interpreters to think that both Reuben and Judah tried to rescue Joseph?

2. Read Genesis 42:21–22. What details in the brothers' own view suggest that they meant evil for Joseph when they sold him?

3. Read Genesis 50:19–20. How does Joseph interpret the intentions of Judah and his brothers for selling him into slavery?

4. Compare Genesis 45:8 (and see context) and 50:20. Why would Joseph interpret evil actions motivated by evil intentions as part of God's plan?

5. What clues help readers know that the narrator of Genesis agrees with Joseph's interpretation of God using evil actions as part of his plan (include three references from Gen 39)?

ACTIVITY 4: *A Close Reading of the Blessing of Judah (A Reading, Genesis 49:8–12)*

1. Underline similar language about the recipient of the blessing and others in the blessing Isaac "accidentally" gave to Jacob and the blessing Jacob gave to Judah.

2. Use broken underlining to mark similar language about the recipient of the blessing and the brothers in the blessing Isaac "accidentally" gave to Jacob and the blessing Jacob gave to Judah.

[Isaac said to Jacob,]

²⁹"May nations serve you

and peoples bow down to you.

Be lord over your brothers,

and may the sons of your mother bow down to you.

May those who curse you be cursed

and those who bless you be blessed." (Gen 27:29)

[Jacob said to Judah,]

⁸"Judah, your brothers will praise you;

your hand will be on the neck of your enemies;

your father's sons will bow down to you.

⁹You are a lion's cub, Judah;

you return from the prey, my son.

Like a lion he crouches and lies down,

like a lioness—who dares to rouse him?

¹⁰The scepter will not depart from Judah,

nor the ruler's staff from between his feet,

until he to whom it belongs shall come

and the obedience of the nations shall be his." (Gen 49:8–10)

3. Compare the blessing of Jacob and the blessing of Judah above. What element in the blessing of Judah indicates that Jacob is advancing the expectations further than Isaac did in the case of the duration of the expected rule of the Judah-king?

4. Why is it important in the context of Genesis to include expectations for the Judah-king to rule over both his brothers and the nations (12:3; 26:4; 28:4)?

    a) The ancestral promise looks ahead to all families of the earth blessed by Abraham

    b) The tribe of Reuben had lost power because of Reuben's sin

    c) Judah was jealous of Joseph's power over pharaoh's kingdom

    d) Judah's first wife was a granddaughter of Ishmael

5. Read Genesis 35:11; 17:16; and 49:10. What imagery in the blessing of Judah indicates Jacob expected a descendant of Judah to be a king like he had been promised?

ACTIVITY 5: *Making It Our Own (The Expected Judah-King in Scripture)*

1. <u>Underline</u> the similarities between the promises to Abraham and Jacob and Balaam's oracle.

2. Use <u>broken underlining</u> to mark the similar language between the blessing of Judah and Balaam's oracle.

> [1]Yahweh had said to Abram, "Go from your country, your people and your father's household to the land I will show you. [2]I will make you into a great nation, and I will bless you; I will make your name great, and you will be a blessing. [3]I will bless those who bless you, and whoever curses you I will curse; and all peoples on earth will be blessed through you." (Gen 12:1–3)

> [Isaac said to Jacob,]
> [29]"May nations serve you
>   and peoples bow down to you.
> Be lord over your brothers,
>   and may the sons of your mother bow down to you.
> May those who curse you be cursed
>   and those who bless you be blessed." (Gen 27:29)

[Jacob said to Judah,]

8"Judah, your brothers will praise you;

> your hand will be on the neck of your enemies;

> your father's sons will bow down to you.

9You are a lion's cub, Judah;

> you return from the prey, my son.

Like a lion he crouches and lies down,

> like a lioness—who dares to rouse him? (Gen 49:8–9)

[Balaam said,] 8"God brought them out of Egypt;

> they have the strength of a wild ox.

They devour hostile nations and break their bones in pieces;

> with their arrows they pierce them.

9Like a lion they crouch and lie down,

> like a lioness—who dares to rouse them?

May those who bless you be blessed

> and those who curse you be cursed!" (Num 24:8–9)

3. How does the oracle of Balaam in Numbers 24:8–9 help confirm that the blessing of Judah carries forward the promises to Abraham?

4. Read 1 Chronicles 28:4 and its context. How does David connect the expectations of Judah to Davidic kingship?

5. In Revelation 5:5–6 and its context, John describes the "_____ of Judah" as the slaughtered _____ (Isa 53:7; John 1:29, 36) and the root of _____, connecting with the imagery of the root of _____ (Isa 11:1, 9). These connections affirm the fulfillment of the Davidic promises and redemptive expectations as fulfillment of the blessing of Judah.

6. Note that the poetic language for donkeys is very precise in the Hebrew of Genesis 49:11 and Zechariah 9:9 but general in the ancient Greek translation of the Hebrew Scriptures known as the Septuagint or LXX. The translation here seeks to clarify these terms. Underline the exact language that Zechariah borrows from the blessing of Judah in his oracle. **Bold** has been used to mark the shared terms in Greek.

7. Use broken underlining to mark similar imagery of tie/untie to the blessing of Judah and Mark 11:1–10. **Bold** has been used to mark the shared terms in Greek.

> [Jacob said,] ¹⁰"The scepter shall not turn aside from Judah, nor the ruler's staff from between his feet, until that which belongs to him **comes**, and the obedience of the peoples is his. ¹¹Tying his jack ("**colt**" in LXX) to the vine, his purebred donkey ("**colt**" in LXX) to a choice vine, he washes his garment in wine, and his robe in the blood of grapes. ¹²His eyes darker than wine, and his teeth whiter than milk." (Gen 49:10–12 lit.)

> ⁹Rejoice greatly, Daughter Zion! Shout, Daughter Jerusalem! See, your king comes to you, righteous and saved, humble and riding on a donkey, on a jack, a purebred donkey ("**young colt**" in LXX). (Zech 9:9 lit.)

> ¹As they approached Jerusalem and came to Bethphage and Bethany at the Mount of Olives, Jesus sent two of his disciples, ²saying to them, "Go to the village ahead of you, and just as you enter it, you will find a **colt** tied there, which no one has ever ridden. Untie it and bring it here. ³If anyone asks you, 'Why are you doing this?' say, 'The Lord needs it and will send it back here shortly.'" ⁴They went and found a **colt** outside in the street, tied at a doorway. As they untied it, ⁵some people standing there asked, "What are you doing, untying that **colt**?" ⁶They answered as Jesus had told them to, and the people let them go. ⁷When they brought the **colt** to Jesus and threw their cloaks over it, he sat on it. ⁸Many people spread their cloaks on the road, while others spread branches they had cut in the fields. ⁹Those who went ahead and those who followed shouted, "Hosanna! Blessed is he who **comes** in the name of the Lord!" ¹⁰"Blessed is the **coming** kingdom of our father David!" "Hosanna in the highest heaven!" (Mark 11:1–10; note that 11:9 is from Ps 118:25, 26)

8. If the Judah-king ties his donkey to the choice _____ when he arrives in Genesis 49:11, then Zechariah identifies the prequel (that which comes before) arriving, namely, the coming of the _____. Zechariah advances the description of the one who rides the donkey by adding that the coming _____ is righteous, _____ (by Yahweh), and _____.

9. Mark encourages his readers to view Messiah as fulfillment of expectation by including echoes of tying and untying from the blessing of Judah and the colt of both the blessing of Judah and the coming _____ of Zechariah.

ACTIVITY 1: *Understanding the Chapter (A Reading, Another Look)*

1. What is the basic problem underlying the story of Exodus?

2. What was the basis of God's salvation of Israel from Egypt?

3. When Israel sins with the golden calf at the base of Mount _____, Moses responds to God's intention of destroying all Israel except _____ by interceding for Israel.

4. What is the culmination of the progressive proximity of Yahweh and Israel in Exodus?
   a) redeeming Israel from physical slavery
   b) revelation of Yahweh's instructions from the mountain
   c) Moses ascending into the cloud on the mountain
   d) Yahweh's glory coming into the dwelling

5. Israel's rebellion with the _____ occupies a grotesque place in the middle of many chapters devoted to _____ for and _____ of Yahweh's dwelling.

6. What great revelation comes in the aftermath of the people's rebellion with the golden calf?

7. Exodus begins with Israel _____ Egypt, inciting oppression, and ends with the glory of Yahweh _____ the dwelling, signaling gracious condescension to reside with his people.

8. Exodus ends with Israel making a _____ for Yahweh's glory, which connects with the beginning of Genesis wherein Yahweh makes a _____ for the humans.

9. What action of the people connects the central wilderness travel sections of Exodus and Numbers?

ACTIVITY 2: *Geography Associated with Exodus (Exodus 1–20)*

For help with geography activities, the best option is a biblical atlas from a library. In addition, many Bibles have maps near the back, or you can use the maps in *Torah Story*.

The geography of the exodus is strongly contested due in large part to inadequate evidence (see Sidebar 13-H: The Reeds Sea and Mount Sinai). For the purposes of this activity simply use the traditional places associated with the exodus from Egypt and the giving of the legal instructions.

1. Write the names of the two cities Israel built, as listed in Exodus 1:11, next to two of the dots on the map.

2. Write the name of the place Israel camped, according to Exodus 12:37, next to one of the dots on the map.

3. Identify three of the possible places of the sea crossing on the map, namely Lake Timsah, the Great Bitter Lake, and the tip of the Gulf of Suez.

4. Write the name of the mountain of revelation, according to Exodus 19:20, next to one of the dots on the map.

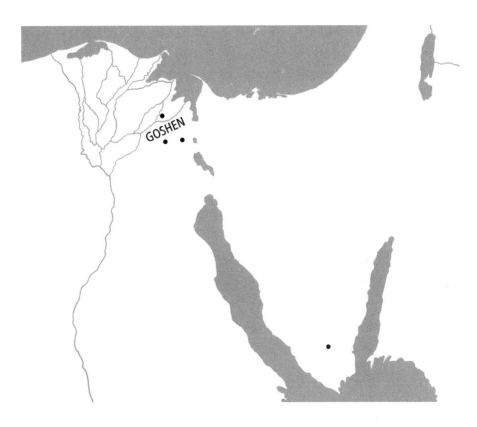

ACTIVITY 3: *Making Connections across Scripture (Another Look)*

1. Place the following items on the correct dotted lines where each fits best to describe both the passages in Exodus on the left and Numbers on the right (one is done for you):

- ○ Moses intercedes
- ○ ~~People complain~~
- ○ People reminisce
- ○ Manna and quail

Exodus			Numbers	
15:23–24	___	...People complain...	11:1	✓
15:25	___	-------------------	11:2	___
16:3	___	-------------------	11:4–6	___
16:13–16	___	-------------------	11:7–9, 31–35	___

2. Now evaluate the passages in Exodus and Numbers on the same themes. Place a check mark on the line on either the Exodus or Numbers side to indicate the worse of the two (one is done for you).

3. What is the significance of the repetition of similar narrative elements in the Exodus and Numbers travel narratives?

ACTIVITY 4: *Making It Our Own (A Reading, Another Look)*

1. Eighty years pass by in Exodus 2 in addition to the suffering of Israel recounted in Exodus 1. What does Exodus 2:23–25 reveal to the people of Israel who lived and died in suffering, thinking they were alone?

2. Compare Exodus 1:22 and 15:1, 4, 21. What is the significance of the imagery of Yahweh throwing the Egyptians into the sea in the Song of the Sea and the song of the women?

3. How does Exodus 34:6–7 reveal the miracle of Yahweh's forgiveness of his people?

12 THE RIVER AND THE BUSH
(Exodus 1–4)

Ryan Faas © 123RF.com

ACTIVITY 1: *Understanding the Chapter (A Reading)*

1. Why does pharaoh seek to exterminate the Hebrew male infants?

  a) Hebrew male children make too much noise

  b) the Hebrews were filling the land

  c) to free up Hebrew females because of an Egyptian shortage

  d) the evidence suggests pharaoh was mentally ill

2. What does not appear in the story of Moses's first forty years?

  a) he is a prince of Egypt

  b) he is adopted by pharaoh's daughter

  c) he is weaned by his own mother

  d) as an infant he could not be hidden more than three months

3. What happens when "God remembers"?

4. What phrase is God's proper name, Yahweh, probably related to?

5. God had not revealed his name to the Hebrew _____ but preserved this honor for _____.

6. During which of Moses's five excuses did God's anger burn against him?

7. When should biblical translations use gender-inclusive language?

  a) always

  b) never

  c) in cases when reference is made to people collectively

  d) not in cases when the Hebrew word is "men" to avoid distortion

53

8. Modern interpreters do well to maintain gender-specific language to preserve the benefits of sons granted to Israel collectively as Yahweh's son because of metaphors like _____ of heart as well as feminine terms to preserve the sense of Israel as _____ of Yahweh.

ACTIVITY 2: *Women Who Deliver (A Reading)*

1. What was the job of the two women who delivered many Hebrew male infants from a deadly anti-Semitic plot?

2. The two women lied to pharaoh and said that Hebrew women are _____.

Matching

3. ___ Zipporah

4. ___ built a little "ark"

5. ___ bathing at the river

6. ___ hiding at the river

7. ___ referred to her husband as "bridegroom of blood"

8. ___ nursed Moses for three months

9. ___ nursed Moses after three months for pay

10. ___ Moses delivered her from predator shepherds

11. ___ performed an emergency circumcision on her son

12. ___ led the first dance in the Bible

A mother of Moses

B sister of Moses

C Pharaoh's daughter

D wife of Moses

13. The savior women provide a literary _____ around the call of Moses.

14. Moses the deliverer was repeatedly _____ by women.

ACTIVITY 3: *Genesis and Exodus (A Reading)*

1. Read Exodus 1:7. What part of Genesis does the description sound like? (choose all that apply)
   a) God's blessing of humans on the sixth creation day
   b) the description of the earth before the first creation day
   c) God's blessing of Noah
   d) God's blessing of the seventh day of rest

2. Exodus 2:2 says that Moses's mother "saw him that he was good" (lit.) in a manner that echoes what God said on which days of creation?

3. Exodus 2:3 says that Moses's mother placed him in an "ark" (lit.). What are the four chapters in Genesis that include the only other uses of the term "ark" (26x) in the Bible?

4. Look up Exodus 10:19; 13:18; 15:4, 22. If you are using the NIV or another modern committee translation, see if these verses have a textual footnote that says the literal name of the body of water is "Sea of Reeds." Read Exodus 2:3, 5. What term does this context use to anticipate the events at the Sea of Reeds?

5. What sort of suggestions do the Genesis-shaped elements of Exodus 1–2 make to the story of the infant delivered among the reeds of the river who will one day lead a people to deliverance at a sea of reeds?

ACTIVITY 4: *Self-Revelation of the God of Israel (A Reading)*

1. The term _____ means four letters. The four letters are __ __ __ __, and they make up the proper name of Israel's God.

2. In ancient times the Hebrew Scriptures were written with only _____ not _____.

3. Originally, Israel would have said the name of their God since it is written in Scripture. During the exile they stopped saying the _____ of Israel's God because it is too holy. Instead, when they read Scripture in Hebrew and came to the name they would say _____, meaning "lord" or "sir," and those who lived in the Greek-speaking diaspora used the Septuagint, which translated the name as _____, also meaning "lord" or "sir."

4. The medieval Judaic secretaries known as the _____ created _____ points and symbols that go with the consonants to mark the traditional synagogue reading of Torah. They did not mark the divine name in Torah according to how it is pronounced, but they used the vowel points and symbols of the alternate Hebrew term _____, meaning "lord" or "sir," since that is what they read aloud when they came to the name.

5. No Masorete would ever read the consonants of the name of Israel's God together with vowels of the alternate Hebrew term _____, meaning "lord" or "sir." Christians misread the term as __ e __ o __ a __ (remember the German Y = J in English and German W = V in English). The traditional Christian word _____ is not the name of God, but the consonants of his name _____ combined with the vowels of the word meaning "lord."

6. Most modern English committee translations like the NIV continue to avoid using the _____ of Israel's God. Instead, they use the term lord with capital "L" and small capital letters "ORD" as "LORD" for the proper name and capital "L" and lowercase "ord" as "Lord" for the Hebrew word _____ when it refers to Israel's God.

ACTIVITY 5: *Making It Our Own (Another Look)*

1. Read Exodus 2:23–25 and 3:6–10. Who does Israel's God say he is? Why does he deliver Israel from oppression?

2. Read Exodus 3:14–15. What are the two ways that Israel's God answers Moses's question: "What is your name?"

3. What are the theological undercurrents of the title of Jesus the Messiah as "Lord" (*kurios*) in the New Testament?

4. Read Exodus 4:22–23; 2 Samuel 7:14; and Matthew 1:23; 3:17. What is the progression of the sense of "son of God" across the Scriptures?

13 THE PLAGUES AND THE SEA
(Exodus 5:1–15:21)

iStock.com/ruvanboshoff

ACTIVITY 1: *Understanding the Chapter (A Reading)*

1. Some biblical interpreters view the ten _____ as directed against ten particular _____ of ancient Egypt. Problems with this approach include multiple functions of Egyptian deities as well as that some Egyptian deities were worshiped only in certain _____ and during certain _____ periods. Ancient Egyptians would not "get it."

2. Read Exodus 12:12; 15:11; 18:11; and Numbers 33:4. These Scriptures explain that Israel's God defeated the Egyptian _____ in general.

3. Which of the ten plagues did God tell Moses he intended to do causing readers to anticipate it even in first reading?

4. How are the ten signs arranged?
   a) two sets of five
   b) three sets of three, plus one
   c) in mirror image format (chiastic)
   d) they are not arranged; they just happened

5. The basic meaning of _____ pharaoh's heart is becoming stubborn or the like. The narrator gives readers an inside look at pharaoh's heart after every _____ plus another three times. The book of Exodus takes an opposite approach to many interpreters who try to downplay or explain what God does to pharaoh—the narrator does not hide it or explain it. Yahweh says, "I have _____ his heart and the hearts of his officials so that I may perform these signs of mine among them that you may tell your _____ and _____ how I dealt harshly with the Egyptians and how I performed my signs among them, and that you may know that I am _____."

59

6. What reason does Scripture record for why God did not lead the Israelites on the shorter path to the promised land?

    a) so they would not change their minds if they faced war

    b) Moses needs to meet his father-in-law

    c) because the Ten Commandments could only be recited at Mount Sinai

    d) the cloud leading them did take the shorter path but Israel went the wrong way

7. The Hebrew *yam suph* was traditionally translated "_____ _____" and identified with the Gulf of Suez, but the term means "_____ of _____." Although its location is unknown, it is large enough to destroy the _____ _____.

ACTIVITY 2: *Cosmic Terrors against Egypt (Table 13-D)*

1. The arrangement of the first nine cosmic terrors against the Egyptians can be evaluated "horizontally" (Table 13-E). Two elements included in terrors 1-2-3 but not in terrors 4-5-6 (see Table 13-D) are Aaron's _____ and pharaoh's _____.

2. The arrangement of the first nine cosmic terrors against the Egyptians can be evaluated "vertically" (Table 13-E). What is the common setting of terrors 1-4-7 (Table 13-D)?

3. What is missing from the setting of terrors 3-6-9 (Table 13-D)?

4. Which of the first nine terrors explicitly do not affect Israel (Table 13-D) (the first one is done for you)? flies (4th), _____, _____, and _____

5. In which two of the accounts of the terrors does pharaoh confess his sin before his heart is hardened (name the plagues)? _____ and _____

Match (answers may be used more than once or not at all)

6. ___ Purpose of cosmic terrors is not merely to get Israel out but to demonstrate Yahweh's uniqueness

7. ___ Egyptians shall know that Israel's God is Yahweh

8. ___ Israel shall know that Israel's God is Yahweh

9. ___ Purpose of letting pharaoh live is to see Yahweh's power

10. ___ Purpose of the cosmic terrors is so pharaoh would refuse and Yahweh would kill his son

A   Exod 4:21–23

B   Exod 6:1–9

C   Exod 7:1–5

D   Exod 9:14–16

ACTIVITY 3: *Sea Crossing (A Reading)*

1. Read Exodus 14:4, 18. Put square brackets [ ] around the account of the fulfillment of what Yahweh predicted in the context below.

2. Read the poetic account of the sea crossing in Exodus 15:10. Put parentheses ( ) around the alternate narrative description of wind in the context below.

3. Read Genesis 8:1. Underline the similar action of God in the sea crossing narrative.

4. Read Genesis 1:9–10. Use dotted underlining to mark the shared imagery in the sea crossing.

5. Use wavy underlining to mark the response of Israel to Yahweh's salvation at the sea.

> [21]Then Moses stretched out his hand over the sea, and all that night Yahweh drove the sea back with a strong east wind and turned it into dry land. The waters were divided, [22]and the Israelites went through the sea on dry ground, with a wall of water on their right and on their left. [23]The Egyptians pursued them, and all Pharaoh's horses and chariots and horsemen followed them into the sea. [24]During the last watch of the night Yahweh looked down from the pillar of fire and cloud at the Egyptian army and threw it into confusion. [25]He jammed the wheels of their chariots so that they had difficulty driving. And the Egyptians said, "Let's get away from the Israelites! Yahweh is fighting for them against Egypt." [26]Then Yahweh said to Moses, "Stretch out your hand over the sea so that the waters may flow back over the Egyptians and their chariots and horsemen." [27]Moses stretched out his hand over the sea, and at daybreak the sea went back to its place. The Egyptians were fleeing toward it, and Yahweh swept them into the sea. [28]The water flowed back and covered the chariots and horsemen—the entire army of Pharaoh that had followed the Israelites into the sea. Not one of them survived. [29]But the Israelites went through the sea on dry ground, with a wall of water on their right and on their left. [30]That day Yahweh saved Israel from the hands of the Egyptians, and Israel saw the Egyptians lying dead on the shore. [31]And when the Israelites saw the mighty hand of Yahweh displayed against the Egyptians, the people feared Yahweh and put their trust in him and in Moses his servant. (Exod 14:21–31)

6. Read Isaiah 43:1, 14–17. Isaiah connects together what two events from Torah to speak of the hope of restoration from exile?

ACTIVITY 4: *Date of the Exodus (Sidebar)*

1. The earlier date of the exodus is _____ BCE. Read 1 Kings 6:1. The narrator situates the beginning of the building of the _____ after the exodus by _____ years.

2. The later date of the exodus is approximately _____ BCE. Read Exodus 1:11. Israel built the cities of Pithom and _____, which was named after pharaoh _____ whose long rule went through most of the _____ BCE.

3. Proponents of the earlier date of the exodus claim _____ is a common name so the city in Exodus 1:11 is not named for the famous pharaoh.

4. Proponents of the later date of the exodus claim that the number _____ in 1 Kings 6:1 is a schematic round number signifying twelve generations of _____ years each. For example, Zadok stands at the midway point of the genealogy of the priests of the First Commonwealth with twelve generations before and after him (1 Chr 6:3–15, see v. 8). Zadok is a contemporary of King _____ (15:11) and King _____ (29:22), setting him at about the time of the building of the _____.

ACTIVITY 5: *Making It Our Own (Another Look)*

1. Read Psalm 77:16–20. What did the sea see that no one else saw?

2. What is the significance of no footprints in Psalm 77:19?

3. Read Psalm 114. What other event does the psalmist connect to the sea crossing? How do these acts of salvation transform Judah and Israel according to the psalmist (114:2)?

4. Read Romans 9:14–18 (note Rom 9:15//Exod 33:19; Rom 9:17//Exod 9:16). How does Paul use the cosmic terrors of Exodus to answer the question of God's justice?

12 THE WILDERNESS AND THE MOUNTAIN
(Exodus 15:22–24:18)

ACTIVITY 1: *Understanding the Chapter (A Reading)*

1. What did the Israelites need during the first of the three grumbling episodes?

   a) water

   b) food

   c) clothing

   d) nothing, ancient Israel complains for no reason

2. Which of these is NOT a name for the laws given in Exodus 20?

   a) Ten Commandments

   b) Decalogue

   c) the greatest commandments

   d) ten words

3. What is the first thing Moses is told to write down?

4. Which of the episodes is out of chronological sequence in Exodus?

   a) sea crossing

   b) complaining in the wilderness

   c) revelation at the mountain

   d) advice for judges from Moses's father-in-law

5. What is distinct about the first five of the ten words?

   a) they lack commandments

   b) they say "Yahweh your God"

   c) they use a different form of the term "Israel"

   d) they correspond to the first five creating days in Genesis 1

6. With what does the Ten Words begin and end?

Matching

7. ___ Ten words		**A**	absolute commands
8. ___ Book of the Covenant		**B**	case laws
9. ___ Apodictic			
10. ___ Casuistic			
11. ___ If *x*, then *y* will be the consequence			

ACTIVITY 2: *Image Commandment (Bible)*

The second commandment in Protestant enumeration draws a lot of attention. The present activity takes notice of a few details in order to prepare the way for later contexts in Torah that rework some of its elements (see later activities).

1. God creates humans in his image, but humans may not make images of God. Put brackets [ ] around the verse that echoes the creation days of Genesis 1.

2. Underline the relational characteristic of God that the second commandment pivots upon.

3. Use broken underlining to mark forbidden relational character demonstrated by image making.

4. Use wavy underlining to mark the relational character Yahweh desires from covenant keepers.

> [4]You shall not make for yourself an image in the form of anything in heaven above or on the earth beneath or in the waters below. [5]You shall not bow down to them or worship them; for I, Yahweh your God, am a jealous God, punishing the children for the sin of the parents to the third and fourth generation of those who hate me, [6]but showing love to a thousand generations of those who love me and keep my commandments. (Exod 20:4–6)

5. What difficult phrase in the second commandment invites interpretations in later biblical contexts (compare Exod 34:6–7, 14–16; Deut 7:9–10)?

ACTIVITY 3: *Name Commandment (A Reading)*

1. What has been the traditional focus of the third commandment?

2. What does it mean that Israel "bears the name of Yahweh"?
   a) Israel belongs to God
   b) Israel represents Yahweh
   c) Yahweh established a covenantal relationship with Israel
   d) the first and third options above
   e) all of the above

3. Read Exodus 28:15–38. The term "bear" appears in verses ___, ___, and ___. The sense of the first use of "bear" in this context is representing _____ when the high priest goes before _____. The engraving on the high priest's forehead is a seal and says _____ ___ _____, meaning the high priest and the people he represents belong to _____.

4. What responsibility does the third commandment place upon those who belong to Yahweh?

ACTIVITY 4: *Covenant Collection in Ancient Near Eastern Context (A Reading)*

1. What two characteristics of legal instructions demonstrate that God is interested in more than mere compliance?

2. The common denominator in a patriarchal setting between the vulnerable classes of _____, _____, and _____ _____ is that they lack a land-owning male.

3. Yahweh is the _____ for the vulnerable classes because he owns the _____.

4. What is the logic of protecting sojourners because you know what it is like to be mistreated?

    a) part of the secret things that belong to God

    b) the eleventh commandment

    c) part of New Testament teaching to repair deficiencies of the law

    d) a golden rule

Matching

5. ___ Cut off hand for striking parent

6. ___ Death penalty for striking parent

7. ___ Death penalty for theft

8. ___ Financial penalty for property crimes

9. ___ Divinely given

10. ___ Dominated by case laws

A law collection of Hammurabi

B covenant collection (Exod 21–23)

C Both

11. What do you think is the most significant implication of the divine origin of biblical law?

ACTIVITY 5: *Making It Our Own (Another Look)*

1. Which one of the first three commandments of the Ten Words (Exod 20:2–3, 4–6, 7) do you think is most disobeyed by Christians today? Why?

2. Read Exodus 22:21–24 and 23:9. How does God's law protect the socially vulnerable classes?

15 THE REBELLION AND THE DWELLING
(Exodus 25–40)

ACTIVITY 1: *Understanding the Chapter (A Reading)*

1. Place the following labels in the correct shaded boxes: • sabbath (2x), • tabernacle • instructions, • tabernacle construction.

2. Place the following on the correct dotted lines: holy space (2x), holy time (2x).

theophany & covenant (19–24)	(25:1–31:11)	(31:12–18)	rebellion & revelation (32–34)	(35:1–3)	(35:4–40:33)
covenant	- - - - - - - - - -	- - - - - - - - - -	renewal	- - - - - - - - - -	- - - - - - - - - -

3. How does the mirror imaging in the narrative structure of Exodus 25–40 enhance the obscene character of the rebellion with the golden calf?

4. Who assists Israel with constructing the dwelling for their God?

5. The dwelling for God needs to be exactly like the _____ he shows to _____ on the mountain.

6. Which item in the tabernacle provided the special locale for the presence of God's glory?

    a) table

    b) ark

    c) lampstand

    d) incense altar

7. What was written on the solid gold plate attached to the high priest's turban?

8. What did the golden calf represent?

    a) Israel's God

    b) an Egyptian god

    c) the sacrifices the people performed

    d) a Canaanite storm god

9. What is the significance of the declaration in plural "These are your gods, Israel, who brought you up out of Egypt" of a singular golden calf in Exodus 32:4?

    a) idolaters are unable to count

    b) they wanted to make more calves but ran out of precious metal

    c) it matches Jeroboam's declaration in 1 Kings 12:28

    d) the golden calf must have had two heads like Canaanite idols

10. If the first dance of the Bible can be characterized as worship (Exod 15:20–21), what may "play" connote in the second dance of the Bible?

11. The figurative language of pharaoh's hard _____ and Israel's stiff _____ both refer to stubborn rebellion against God.

12. What made the difference between the way God dealt with pharaoh and the way he dealt with Israel?

    a) Israel repented but pharaoh did not

    b) Moses interceded for Israel

    c) the word of God

    d) God treats everyone the same

ACTIVITY 2: *Dwelling (A Reading)*

1. On the solid lines place the following labels of the correct areas of the dwelling: • outer court, • holy place, and • holy of holies.

2. On the dotted lines place the following labels to identify the furniture of the dwelling: • ark, • bronze basin, • bronze altar, • incense altar, • lampstand, and • table for shewbread.

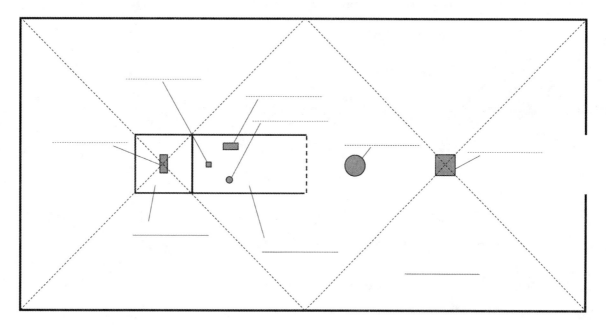

3. What does the dwelling of God represent?

4. How does the dwelling support the idea of graduated holiness in worship?

ACTIVITY 3: *Intercession (A Reading, Bible)*

1. First-person discourse means to speak of oneself (I, me, we, us), second person to directly address another (you), and third person to talk about another (she, he, it, they, them, their). In Exodus 32:7–14 below, underline the places Yahweh uses second-person language of Moses's people and redemption.

2. Use broken underlining to mark the places in Exodus 32:7–14 that Moses uses second-person language of Yahweh's people.

3. Why do Moses and Yahweh characterize Israel differently?

⁷Then Yahweh said to Moses, "Go down, because your people, whom you brought up out of Egypt, have become corrupt. ⁸They have been quick to turn away from what I commanded them and have made themselves an idol cast in the shape of a calf. They have bowed down to it and sacrificed to it and have said, 'These are your gods, Israel, who brought you up out of Egypt.' ⁹I have seen these people," Yahweh said to Moses, "and they are a stiff-necked people. ¹⁰Now leave me alone so that my anger may burn against them and that I may destroy them. Then I will make you into a great nation."

¹¹But Moses sought the favor of Yahweh his God. "Yahweh," he said, "why should your anger burn against your people, whom you brought out of Egypt with great power and a mighty hand? ¹²Why should the Egyptians say, 'It was with evil intent that he brought them out, to kill them in the mountains and to wipe them off the face of the earth'? Turn from your fierce anger; relent and do not bring disaster on your people. ¹³Remember your servants Abraham, Isaac and Israel, to whom you swore by your own self: 'I will make your descendants as numerous as the stars in the sky and I will give your descendants all this land I promised them, and it will be their inheritance forever.'"

¹⁴Then Yahweh relented and did not bring on his people the disaster he had threatened. (Exod 32:7–14)

4. In Moses's intercession in Exodus 32:7–14 above, put brackets [ ] around the place(s) Moses alludes to God's rationale for his signs as expressed in Exodus 7:1–5 and 14:4, 15–18.

5. In Moses's intercession in Exodus 32:7–14 above, put parentheses ( ) around the place(s) Moses alludes to God's rationale for his deliverance of Israel in Exodus 2:23–25 and 3:7–10.

6. What is the importance of Moses referring to Yahweh's own rationale in a prayer to Yahweh himself?

7. What kind of hope does Exodus 32:14 offer? What about Exodus 32:14 troubles Christian interpreters?

ACTIVITY 4: *Renewal (A Reading)*

1. Read Exodus 33:1–3. Why does Yahweh decide not to go with Israel (choose one)? wrath or mercy

2. Read Exodus 33:12–19. Why does Yahweh decide to go with Israel (choose one)? wrath or mercy

As noted in a previous activity (see Chapter 14, Activity 2), the threat of multigenerational judgment was a great concern for biblical authors. This even includes concern for interpretation of it within the Exodus itself.

3. Underline the exact verbal parallels between Exodus 20:4–6 and 34:6–7.

4. Use broken underlining (in a different color if possible) to mark exact verbal parallels between Exodus 20:4–6 and 34:14–16.

²I am Yahweh your God, who brought you out of Egypt, out of the land of slavery. ³You shall have no other gods before me.

⁴You shall not make for yourself an image in the form of anything in heaven above or on the earth beneath or in the waters below. ⁵You shall not bow down to them or serve them; for I, Yahweh your God, am a jealous God, punishing the iniquity of the parents upon the children to the third and fourth generation of those who hate me, ⁶but showing loyalty to thousands of those who love me and keep my commandments. (Exod 20:2–6, vv. 5–6 lit.)

⁶And he passed in front of Moses, calling out, "Yahweh, Yahweh, a God compassionate and gracious, slow to anger, abounding in loyalty and faithfulness, ⁷maintaining loyalty to thousands, and forgiving iniquity, transgression, and sin. Yet he does not leave the guilty unpunished; punishing the iniquity of the parents upon the children and upon the grandchildren to the third and fourth generation. (Exod 34:6–7 lit.)

¹⁴You shall not bow down to another god, for Yahweh, whose name is Jealous, he is a jealous God. ¹⁵Be careful lest you make a covenant with those who live in the land; for when they prostitute themselves to their gods and sacrifice to them, they will invite you and you will eat their sacrifices. ¹⁶And when you take some of their daughters for your sons and those daughters prostitute themselves to their gods, they will lead your sons to prostitute themselves to their gods. (Exod 34:14–16 lit.)

5. In the attribute formula of the revelation in Exodus 34:6–7, God says he is _____ and _____ —in comparison to a _____ God in the image commandment of Exodus 20:4–6. In the covenant renewal of Exodus 34:11–26 (here focused on vv. 14–16), what characterizes God so much that it is his name? _____

6. The daughter-in-law from the land makes her Israelite husband into a _____ after the gods of the land. Such a couple will likely have children who worship other _____.

7. If the parents arrange marriage for their sons to become prostitutes after gods of the land, at least how many generations participate in false worship? _____

8. How does the multigenerational rebellion of apostasy marriages in Exodus 34:14–16 help explain who is at fault with regard to the multigenerational wrath threatened in the image commandment (Exod 20:5) and the attribute formula (34:7)?
  a) only the parents sin by arranging the apostasy marriage
  b) only the children sin by acting as prostitutes to false gods
  c) both parents and children (and potential grandchildren) actively participate in rebellion
  d) neither parents nor children sin if the apostasy marriage helps them financially and socially in a challenging culture

ACTIVITY 5: *Making It Our Own (Another Look)*

1. Why does the revelation and covenant renewal in Exodus 34 offer hope to the people of God?

2. Who is at risk in the prohibition and warning at the beginning of the covenant renewal in Exodus 34:11–16?

3. Read Exodus 32:12–14 and Jonah 3:9–10. Now read Exodus 34:6 and Jonah 4:2. Why is Jonah angry with Yahweh?

16 MACROVIEW OF LEVITICUS

ACTIVITY 1: *Understanding the Chapter (A Reading)*

1. What is the book of Leviticus about?

    a) instructions for living in light of God's glory dwelling with Israel

    b) Levites

    c) Levites and Levitical cities

    d) instructions for building the tabernacle

2. The leading idea in Leviticus is the _____ of God.

3. "Holy" in Leviticus refers to being set _____ toward _____.

4. What does it mean to say the dwelling is a microcosm of creation?

    a) the dwelling in the camp is like the world writ small

    b) the microorganisms in unclean food are unhealthy

    c) the curtains of the holy of holies can be considered an ancient microfiber

    d) humans seem small and insignificant compared to God

5. The ritual purity standards of Leviticus 11–15 mean that _____ at any _____ is liable to ritual pollution.

6. The problem of _____ in Leviticus stems from God's glory taking up residence with Israel. God's holy dwelling is _____ because of Israel's stubbornness.

7. Why was the gift of God's instruction needed for survival in the newly established holy space?

    a) the purpose of the law is to control Israel

    b) the purpose of the law is unquestioning compliance, not relationship by grace

    c) an unholy people could ritually pollute God's holy dwelling

    d) the building of the tabernacle put an end to manna

8. The first half of Leviticus focuses on purity for the _____ within the community. The second half is oriented toward _____ for persons within the community of God's people.

9. Between backward-looking Genesis and forward-looking _____, Leviticus emerges as the _____ panel of Torah.

10. What two books along with Leviticus make up the wilderness series?

    a) Genesis and Exodus

    b) Genesis and Numbers

    c) Exodus and Numbers

    d) Numbers and Deuteronomy

11. What is the controlling genre of Leviticus?

    a) law

    b) legalistic regulations opposed to the Holy Spirit

    c) lists of regulations

    d) story

Match Leviticus narrative framing

12. ____ Sacrifice (Lev 1–7)

13. ____ Death of Nadab and Abihu (10:1–2)

14. ____ Forbidden relations (18)

15. ____ Sabbath year and Jubilee Year (25)

A Punishments for forbidden relations (Lev 20)

B Death of Aaron's sons (16:1)

C Vows and tithes (27)

D Day of Atonement (16)

ACTIVITY 2: *Leviticus as Genesis-shaped (A Reading)*

Matching

1. ____ Ritually clean and unclean animals (Lev 11)

2. ____ Circumcision on the eighth day (Lev 12:3)

3. ____ Prohibition against consuming blood (Lev 17:10–14)

4. ____ Pollutions of the peoples of Canaan (Lev 18:24–30)

5. ____ Sabbath rest (Lev 23:3)

6. ____ Division of times (Lev 23:2, 4)

A Genesis 1:14–19

B Genesis 2:2–3

C Genesis 7:2

D Genesis 9:4

E Genesis 15:16

F Genesis 17:9–14

ACTIVITY 3: *Making It Our Own (Another Look)*

1. Read Exodus 33:3–5. How does the dangerous presence of God with Israel cause the instructions of Leviticus to be a gift of Yahweh's mercy?

2. Read Leviticus 10:6 and 21:1–6, 10–11. Why does Yahweh expect priests to have non-torn garments and neat hair?

3. Read Leviticus 19:1–2; 1 Peter 1:15–16; and Numbers 16:1–3. If Israel and Christians are called to be holy, what is wrong with what Korah, Dathan, Abiram, and On said in Numbers 16:3?

17 SACRIFICE
(Leviticus 1–7)

ACTIVITY 1: *Understanding the Chapter (A Reading)*

1. What makes understanding sacrifices difficult?

 a) Leviticus has too many regulations

 b) it requires imagination because it is not currently operational

 c) the standards for sacrifice appeal only to legalistic people

 d) sacrifices were designed as an obstacle to turn people to the Holy Spirit

2. Sometimes Christian preaching uses too much zeal in over-imaginative ways that the tabernacle or _____ might _____ the Messiah.

3. What is different about the sort of logic needed to apprehend sacrifice?

 a) analogical associations are governed by "like" or "as" resemblances

 b) Hebrew thought is different than Greek thought

 c) details of sacrifice are best viewed analytically like an anatomy textbook would view them

 d) they use linear rational deduction and induction

4. What is the purpose of animal sacrifices in Leviticus?

 a) temporarily cover sin by works

 b) celebrate microcosmic depictions of the biblical worldview

 c) literally pay for sin by blood

 d) provide a different way of salvation by good works

5. The problem with the term "_____" (*hatta't*) to describe the "_____ offering"—or better "purification offering"—is that this offering was not for _____ but ritual contamination. The sorts of situations that requires purification offering are: individual _____ sin (Lev 4:2), collective _____ sin (4:13), coming in contact with a ritually _____ animal or person (5:2–3), giving _____ to a child (12:6–8), male _____ (15:15), _____ relations (15:18), and female _____ (15:30). The use of the Hebrew term "sin" (*hatta't*) includes ritual impairments that are not moral and often not intentional. This stands in contrast to the Protestant Christian theological use of the term to speak to immoral attitudes, thoughts, and actions, or the absence of doing what is right. In sum, the so-called _____ offering is not for things that Protestants consider _____. Thus, a functional term like _____ offering better gets at its role in purifying ritual impairments like childbirth, menstruation, or male flow.

6. Read Leviticus 12:6–8 and Luke 2:22–24. It was not a _____ for _____ the mother of the Messiah to give birth to a son. The purification offering is part of her obedience for the ritual disability caused by a natural bodily function.

Match the best answer (answers may be used more than once or not at all)

7. ___ Voluntary		A	Burnt offering
8. ___ Mandatory		B	Grain offering
9. ___ Of no value		C	Well-being offering
10. ___ Temporary payment for sin		D	A, B, and C
11. ___ Symbolic of the faith, obedience, and devotion of the worshiper		E	Purification offering
12. ___ Pleasing aroma of gratitude of the worshiper		F	Reparation offering
13. ___ For ritual impairments and unintentional transgressions		G	E and F
14. ___ Traditionally known as "guilt" offering		H	All of the above
15. ___ Traditionally known as "sin" offering		I	None of the above
16. ___ Offender paid back victim plus twenty percent			
17. ___ Could be eaten by laity			
18. ___ Mandatory offering with economical alternates for financially challenged persons			

ACTIVITY 2: *Analogical Relations (A Reading)*

1. The priest viewed animal sacrifices from an _____ point of view—the slain animal is turned over with the legs up.

2. The middle part of an animal sacrifice includes the _____, _____ on them, and the lobe of the _____ (Lev 3:15). All the _____ belongs to Yahweh (3:16). These internal organs may symbolize the inmost _____ of the soul that are in the purview of _____ alone (Jer 17:9–10).

3. The lower portion of the animal sacrifice is the _____, which could be eaten in the case of the well-being offering by the priest and the people. The upper part of the sacrifice is the _____, _____, and _____ organ, which belong to Yahweh alone. Perhaps the _____ organ belongs to Yahweh as a symbol of fertility and life.

4. Compare the graduated holiness of the mountain of revelation, the tabernacle, and the animal sacrifice. On the appropriate dotted lines of the mountain icon place the name of the one person who had access to the top (Exod 24:15), those who had could ascend part way up (24:9), and those whom God brought to the base of the mountain (19:17).

5. On the appropriate dotted lines of the tabernacle icon place • the title of the one person who had access to the holy of holies (Lev 16:15), • those who could come into the holy place to serve (Exod 28:43), • and those who sacrifice their animals at the entrance of the tabernacle (Lev 1:2, etc.).

6. On the appropriate dotted lines of the animal sacrifice icon list • "head and body," • the elements that make up the middle part of the sacrifice (Lev 3:15), and • the elements of the top part (1:13; 3:9).

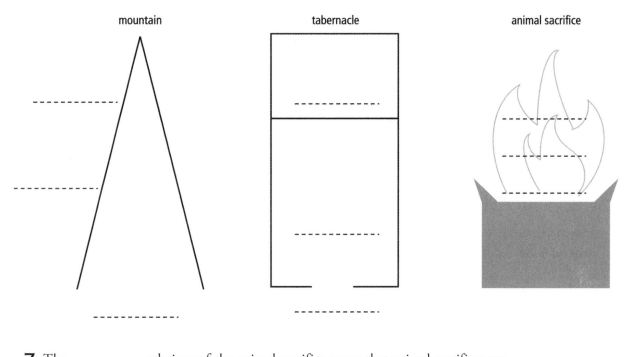

7. The _____ relations of the animal sacrifice mean that animal sacrifices are _____ representations of the universe. Every sacrifice celebrates graduated _____ wherein coming into closer proximity to God is available to fewer people of his choosing within an increasingly dangerous holy space.

ACTIVITY 3: *Reparation Offering (A Reading)*

1. Read Numbers 15:30–31. The teaching on "high-handed" or defiant sin with no sacrifice leads some interpreters to view the guilt or reparation offering as only for what kind of sins?

    a) unintentional transgressions

    b) intentional transgressions

    c) both

2. Read Leviticus 19:20–22. The case law includes several social dynamics to protect the weaker party who is a _____ engaged to another. The transgressor who has _____ relations that are *definitely intentional* is able to make a _____ offering to get right with the person who was wronged and be _____ by God. This indicates that the reasons for a reparation offering, inclusive of accidental and _____ sins, is to help one get right with one's fellow and with God.

3. When the teaching of the _____-_____ sin for which there is no forgiveness (Num 15:30–31 ESV) is put together with the _____ offering (Lev 6:1–7), which can serve as a vehicle for repentance for God's forgiveness (19:20–22), it means that the person who sins with a high-hand and refuses to _____ cannot be forgiven.

ACTIVITY 4: *Making It Our Own (Another Look)*

1. Read Psalm 51:18–19. Under what conditions does God delight in sacrifices?

2. Read Psalm 51:16–17. According to Psalm 51:17, what kind of heart attitude are sacrifices intended to symbolize?

18 PURITY AND WORSHIP
(Leviticus 8–16)

ACTIVITY 1: *Understanding the Chapter (A Reading)*

1. The privilege of close proximity to God's glory with the _____ comes with the responsibilities of his dangerous _____.

2. Who is the first messiah in the Bible?

3. Leviticus is a narrative of instructions for _____ and _____. Leviticus contains only two narrative episodes: the institution of the _____ and the execution of the _____. In both narrative episodes people die: _____ and _____ for unauthorized fire in Leviticus 10 and the precedent-setting execution by _____ of the law breaker in Leviticus 24:10–23. That both of the narrative episodes include people dying for rebellion reinforces the danger of Yahweh's holiness.

4. The ritual clean and ritual unclean standards in Leviticus 11–15 progress from things outside (_____) to things that touch (corpses) to things from a person (childbirth) to things on a person (_____ _____) to things that come from inside a person (_____). This progression corresponds to the ritual purification of the Day of _____, beginning in the _____ of _____ and moving outward (Lev 16).

5. Which of the animal groups does not have a physical criterion to label them as ritually clean or unclean?
  a) land animals
  b) water animals
  c) swarming insects
  d) birds

6. What is the traditional view of ceremonially unclean and ceremonially clean dictary regulations—the only view that is not internally inconsistent with known evidence?
  a) unclean animals and states refer to dirt or repugnant elements
  b) unclean animals are unhealthy and foster poor hygiene
  c) declaring some animals unclean protects them from indiscriminate consumption
  d) unclean animals are so because God said so

7. The problem with translating the Hebrew word *tsara'at* as _____ is that it cannot refer to Hansen's disease. The reasons include that _____ (Lev 13:47–59) and _____ (14:33–53) cannot get Hansen's disease. Thus, Hansen's disease is one of many _____ _____ that falls within the range of *tsara'at*— some are incurable like Hansen's disease and others are temporary.

8. What are two common ways to understand the Hebrew term *'aza'zel* in the Day of Atonement regulations (Lev 6:8, 10, 26)? (choose two)

    a) scapegoat

    b) sacrificial goat

    c) name of a desert demon

    d) the name of the stream in the desert near the tabernacle when it was at Mount Sinai

9. What is one of the major purposes of the Day of Atonement (Lev 16:33–34)?

    a) cleansing the tabernacle from ritual contamination

    b) personal forgiveness for individuals from sins of immorality

    c) the need for a religious holiday to take off of work

    d) a publicly sanctioned mechanism to dispose of nuisance goats

10. What is the authoritative meaning of Messiah's new torah: "whatever goes into a person from the outside cannot defile" (Mark 7:19)?

    a) people need to be discriminating of the ingredients of prepared food

    b) people should avoid overeating

    c) it is important to finish food since the poor do not have enough

    d) all foods are ceremonially clean

ACTIVITY 2: *Overlap of Ritual, Holy, and Moral Standards (A Reading)*

1. The concepts of ritually clean/ritually _____ versus holy/_____ versus righteous/_____ can be challenging because they overlap in everyday life. The three ideas of ritually clean, holy, and righteous speak to different things. For this reason a person can commit sin and remain ritually clean and holy while someone else may become ritually unclean on purpose as an act of righteousness.

In the case studies that follow, **put a check mark** in each category that applies. The first one is completed as an example: When a woman of Israel steals, she has sinned and has become unholy in a relative sense, meaning she is unfit to worship because of the sin that impairs her relationship with God, even while she remains holy in a categorical sense in that she remains a part of Israel set apart from the nations.

	ritually unclean	holy in a categorical sense	unholy in a relative sense	sinful	a righteous act
A woman of Israel steals (Exod 20:15).	--	✓	✓	✓	--
2. A woman of Israel gives birth to a female child (Lev 12:5).					
3. A Levite helps bury his deceased father-in-law (Num 19:11; cf. Lev 21:1–4, 11).					
4. A married couple of Israel has conjugal relations (Lev 15:18).					
5. A priest eats a roasted locust (Lev 11:22).					
6. A Levite's wife eats a white owl (Lev 11:17).					
7. A man of Israel acquires a skin disease (Lev 13).					
8. A Levite eats bacon and eggs (Lev 11:7).					
9. A man of Israel with a discharge respects an elder (Lev 15:1–15; 19:32).					
10. An Israelite wife does not sit on the chair after her husband with a discharge sits on it (Lev 15:6).					
11. A new mother of Israel refuses to make a purification offering after giving birth to a male child (Lev 12:6–8).					
Challenge case study:					
12. A woman of Israel who is menstruating touches the donkey of her enemy while trying to help it from its burden. Her enemy warns that the donkey is dying. Yet the woman continues to help it, still touching it when it dies. See Exod 23:5; Lev 11:8; 15:19–24; cf. Exod 13:13 with Num 18:15.					

ACTIVITY 3: *Sacrifices and the Sacrifice of Messiah (A Reading)*

Many Christians do well to apprehend that Messiah's death takes care of all sacrifices once and for all. Too well. Based upon this some Christians do not bother thinking through the different functions of sacrifices to learn all of what Messiah has accomplished in his death. The present activity reviews the purposes of three different sacrifices in order to appreciate what Messiah's death and resurrection accomplishes for followers of Messiah.

1. **Passover.** Read Exodus 12:21–27. The purpose of the Passover lamb is (choose one) for sin or a substitute for the firstborn. Read Exodus 12:46; Psalm 34:19–20; and John 19:31–36. When Messiah's bones were not broken, it suggests the _____ lamb serves as a figural expectation fulfilled in the death of Messiah.

2. **Day of Atonement.** Review the purposes of the so-called sin or purification offering in *Workbook* Chapter 17, activity 1, number 5 (p. 79). Read Leviticus 16:15. The kind of sacrifice serving as the centerpiece of the Day of Atonement is the _____ offering. The purpose of the Day of Atonement is to cleanse the _____ (Lev 16:16) from ritual pollutions in order for Yahweh to maintain covenantal relations dwelling among his people. According to Hebrews 10:19–25, the _____ of Messiah opens access for his followers to _____ God in faith.

3. **Reparation offering.** Review the purposes of the so-called reparation or guilt offering in *Workbook* Chapter 17, activity 3 (p. 81). The reparation offering is to repent of sin—intentional or unintentional—to get right with one's fellow and be _____ by God. The servant is a guilt or reparation offering for _____ (Isa 53:10). His sacrifice for sin is offered on behalf of our _____ and _____ (53:5). Compare Isaiah 53 and 1 Peter 2:24–25. In the spaces provided list the verse references from Isaiah 53 that are alluded to in the following passage: [24] "'He himself bore our sins'" in his body on the cross, so that we might die to sins and live for righteousness; 'by his wounds you have been healed' [**Isa 53:** __]. [25] For 'you were like sheep going astray' [**Isa 53:** __], but now you have returned to the Shepherd and Overseer of your souls" (1 Pet 2:24–25).

ACTIVITY 4: *Making It Our Own (Another Look)*

1. Read Leviticus 9:24; 1 Chronicles 21:26; and 2 Chronicles 7:1. What is significant about these three events that triggers fire from the realm of Yahweh?

2. Read Leviticus 10:10–11. How does the context bear on the priestly responsibility to instruct Israel in ways of worship?

19 HOLY LIVING
(Leviticus 17–27)

ACTIVITY 1: *Understanding the Chapter (A Reading)*

1. The focus of Leviticus 17–26 is upon the holiness of (choose one) individual persons or members of the community.

2. Leviticus 17–26 is often referred to as the _____ collection.

3. What does blood symbolize? _____

4. The repeated phrase "do not uncover the _____ of X" (lit.) is a _____ for sexual relations. The set of prohibited incestuous relations in Leviticus 18:6–18 infers the basic _____ structure. Leviticus 20:11–12, 14, 17, 19–21 explains the criminal _____ of violating the prohibitions against incest.

5. A literary _____ can be used to effectively draw greater attention to that which is omitted. This seems to be the case for not listing the prohibition against having relations with a _____ even while the blanket statement in Leviticus 18:6 says any close relative who are elsewhere defined as "his mother or father, his son or _____, his brother . . ." (Lev 21:2).

6. What are ways the second half of Leviticus personifies the land of promise? (choose all that apply)
   a) defilement by the nations causes the land's nausea and vomiting
   b) disobedience by Israel causes the land's nausea and vomiting
   c) fruit trees of the land must be circumcised
   d) the land prowls about like a lion seeking someone to devour
   e) the land must take Sabbath rest

7. What is the common denominator of the sixteen laws in Leviticus 19 that include the phrase "I am Yahweh (your God)"?
   a) the legal standards could be violated in secret
   b) the legal standards also appear in the Ten Commandments
   c) the legal standards also appear in the New Testament
   d) there is no common denominator

8. What is the final stage of judgment that God promises if the people do not listen to him?

9. What does the figure of a circumcised heart in Leviticus 26:40–41 refer to?

ACTIVITY 2: *Purity Standards (A Reading)*

In addition to forbidden incestuous relations between family members—"Do not uncover the nakedness of" (ESV) or "do not have sexual relations with" (NIV)—what six **other** sexual sins are prohibited in Leviticus 18–20? (Since one is done already you only need to identify five more, including references, prohibited acts, and reasons.)

	prohibition	reference of prohibition		punishment or consequence	reference of punishment
1.			→		
2.			→		
3.			→		
4.			→		
	• fornication with a slave betrothed to another	19:20–22	→	reparation offering (compensation plus 20 percent)	19:20b–21; cf. 6:5
5.			→		

6. Whether or not one believes there are biblical grounds for considering some sexual sins worse than others, the treatment of persons who practice different kinds of sexual misconduct should not be driven by hateful prejudice. Based on your work above, what three sexual sins are punished with same severity (capital punishment)?

7. Since the three sexual sins listed above each require the same punishment, how should Christians treat those caught in or repentant of these acts of sexual misconduct in comparison to one another?

8. Another way some Christians have treated certain acts of sexual misconduct worse than others is to focus on the wording of laws in Leviticus 18. They say because the prohibition against same-sex relations in Leviticus 18:22 uses the expression "That is detestable" (NIV) or "It is an abomination" (ESV), it is worse than other sexual sins. The term translated "detestable" (NIV) or "abomination" (ESV) is the Hebrew word *to'evah* (plural: *to'evot*). Circle all of the uses of this term in the following passage in the NIV:

> ²⁶But you must keep my decrees and my laws. The native-born and the foreigners residing among you must not do any of these detestable things, ²⁷for all these things were done by the people who lived in the land before you, and the land became defiled. ²⁸And if you defile the land, it will vomit you out as it vomited out the nations that were before you. ²⁹Everyone who does any of these detestable things—such persons must be cut off from their people. ³⁰Keep my requirements and do not follow any of the detestable customs that were practiced before you came and do not defile yourselves with them. I am Yahweh your God. (Lev 18:26–30)

9. Based on the use of the term "detestable" (*to'evah/to'evot*) in Leviticus 18:26–30, does this context treat a particular sexual sin as worse than others or does it treat all sorts of sexual sin in the same way? What does this tell us about the importance of sexual purity? Explain.

10. What kinds of social circumstances protect the weaker party in the non-capital crimes of sexual misconduct (including Scripture references[s])?

11. Why is sexual purity so important in Leviticus 18–20 (include Scripture reference[s])?

ACTIVITY 3: *Love Thy Neighbor (A Reading)*

1. Review. <u>Underline</u> the similar themes in Exodus 22:21 and 23:9.

> Do not mistreat or oppress a foreigner, for you were foreigners in Egypt. (Exod 22:21)

> Do not oppress a foreigner; you yourselves know how it feels to be foreigners, because you were foreigners in Egypt. (Exod 23:9)

2. How does Exodus 23:9 explain the underlying reason for the prohibition against abusing residing foreigners?

3. Use <u>broken underlining</u> to mark the verbal parallels in Exodus 22:21 and Leviticus 19:33–34.

4. Use <u>wavy underlining</u> to mark the verbal parallels in Leviticus 19:33–34 and 19:18.

> Do not mistreat or oppress a residing foreigner, for you were residing foreigners in the land of Egypt. (Exod 22:21 lit.)

> [33]When a residing foreigner resides among you in your land, do not mistreat them. [34]The residing foreigner residing among you must be treated as your native-born. Love them as yourself, for you were residing foreigners in Egypt. I am Yahweh your God. (Lev 19:33–34 lit.)

> Do not seek revenge or bear a grudge against anyone among your people, but love your neighbor as yourself. I am Yahweh. (19:18)

5. How does Leviticus 19:33–34 advance the responsibilities of Israel toward others among them in Exodus 22:21?

6. How does Leviticus 19:18 take the next step to advance the instructions in 19:33–34?

ACTIVITY 4: *Making It Our Own (Another Look)*

1. Select one of the *social* laws in Leviticus 19 that includes the phrase "I am Yahweh" or "I am Yahweh your God." What is one example of a *social* standard in Leviticus 19 that would be impossible to legislate in court? Why? How does "I am Yahweh (your God)" provide a rationale?

2. Read Leviticus 26:40–45. How does Yahweh promise to respond to the humble confession of Israel when they are suffering in exile?

20 MACROVIEW OF NUMBERS

ACTIVITY 1: *Understanding the Chapter (A Reading)*

1. Whereas the traditional Christian name of the book of "_____" refers to the genealogies of the first and second generation of Israel, the traditional Judaic name "____ ____ _____" gets at the setting of the narrative.

2. In a general chronology of Exodus through Deuteronomy, the greatest proportion of biblical text focuses on Israel at two places, namely, at the mountain (especially with instructions in Exodus and _____), and on the plains of _____ (especially with instructions in _____). By contrast, the greatest amount of time elapses in the middle few chapters of _____ in the wilderness.

3. What are the only narratives to illuminate the thirty-eight "silent years"?
    a) snakes and the bronze snake on the pole
    b) Korah's rebellion and the budding of Aaron's staff
    c) Moses's and Aaron's sin
    d) counting the second generation in a military census and their battles

Match spaces of numbers (letters A–E) with their narrative symbolic functions

4. ___ Hope for future residence
5. ___ Fictive memories of the good old days
6. ___ Present testing
7. ___ Revelation of God
8. ___ Mortal and moral enemy

A Egypt
B Mount Sinai
C the wilderness
D Moab
E Canaan

9. Who rescues the second generation of Israelites from severe threats?
    a) Balaam and Aaron
    b) Moses and Jethro
    c) God and Phinehas
    d) Moses and Zipporah

10. Exodus and Numbers narrate _____ travels and three encampments at Sinai, Kadesh, and the plains of Moab out of _____ stops from Egypt to the land of promise.

11. The first generation of the redeemed community died in the _____, and the second generation entered into the land of _____.

12. The repetitious narrative structure of Numbers demonstrates something about Yahweh, Israel, and the wilderness. The repeated grumblings and rebellions demonstrate Yahweh as something like a gracious _____ (Deut 8:5). The story of two generations of Israel in the wilderness illustrates their addiction to _____. The wilderness shows the people that it was never really the problem because Yahweh sustained them—Israel does not live on bread only but on every _____ from Yahweh (Deut 8:3).

13. What is the character of the inner-tribal relations and larger social world of Numbers?
   a) Genesis-shaped
   b) conflict and chaos
   c) sin and grumbling
   d) revealed by Balaam the prophet

ACTIVITY 2: *Name That Genre (A Reading, Numbers 1–36)*

The purpose of this activity is to become broadly familiar with the many literary genres of Numbers and the book's general arrangement. Use *Torah Story* and especially Numbers 1–36.

1. On each blank, label the basic genre of the unit with the best fit (use different colors for each genre if possible):
   List = archival list (census, arrangements, itemized reports, etc.);
   Law = law or legal ruling;
   NN = non-storyline narrative;
   S = storyline narrative

_____	1	census
_____	2	arrangement of camp
_____	3, 4	census arrangement, roles of Levites
_____	5	regulations on suspected adulteress
_____	6	Nazirite vows
List	7	dedication of tabernacle report
_____	8	regulations and dedication of Levites
Law	9:1–14	alternate Passover regulations
NN	9:15–10:10	routine of tabernacle moving
_____	10:11–12:16	wilderness travels narrative
_____	13–14	Kadesh camp narrative
_____	15	various regulations (7x, including tassels, high-handed sin)

_____	**16**	rebellion of Korah and associates
_____	**17**	plague and Aaron's staff
_____	**18**	regulations for priests and Levites
_____	**19**	regulation of red heifer
_____	**20, 21**	travel narratives and military reports
NN	**22–24**	Balaam narratives
_____	**25**	rebellion at Shittim narrative
_____	**26**	census of the second generation
_____	**27:1–11**	ruling on Zelophehad's daughters
S	**27:12–23**	Joshua chosen as successor
_____	**28, 29**	festival regulations
_____	**30**	on vows
S	**31:1–24**	military report on battle against Midian/Moab
_____	**31:25–54**	inventory of spoils
S	**32**	Transjordan tribes' proposal
_____	**33**	travel itinerary
_____	**34**	apportioning the land
_____	**35**	Levitical towns and related matters
_____	**36**	ruling on Zelophehad's daughters' inheritance

2. In one sentence, what is the significance and narrative function of so many archival lists (see no. 1 above) embedded as artifacts within Numbers?

3. With several long and short legal collections already in Torah—ten words (Exod 20//Deut 5), covenant collection (21–23), renewal collection (34:11–26), priestly standards (Lev 1–7, 11–16, 27), holiness collection (17–26), torah collection (Deut 12–26)—it is interesting that the laws and legal rulings of Numbers (see no. 1 above) have not been collated into these other legal collections. In one sentence, what is the effect of embedding laws and legal rulings throughout the Numbers narrative?

4. Storyline narratives include about twelve of thirty-six chapters of Numbers—about one-third. Look back at the list of storyline narratives you marked in number 1 above. In one sentence, why do the storyline narratives offer the crucial element in an overall interpretation of the function of Numbers?

ACTIVITY 3: *Timeline (Another Look)*

1. Under the Sinai and Moab sections below, in the blanks provided list how much time elapsed for each segment.

2. Circle one of the three portions of the wilderness narrative during which the most time elapses and list the length of time under it.

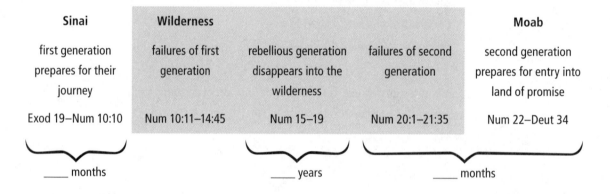

Sinai	Wilderness			Moab
first generation prepares for their journey	failures of first generation	rebellious generation disappears into the wilderness	failures of second generation	second generation prepares for entry into land of promise
Exod 19–Num 10:10	Num 10:11–14:45	Num 15–19	Num 20:1–21:35	Num 22–Deut 34

_____ months   _____ years   _____ months

ACTIVITY 4: *Making It Our Own (Another Look)*

1. Read Numbers 27:16–23. What was Israel's situation without Moses? What characterizes his replacement?

2. Read Numbers 32:13–15. How did the younger generation of Israel compare to the older generation? What are the implications of this comparison regarding Israel and regarding God?

21 THE FIRST GENERATION AT SINAI
(Numbers 1:1–10:10)

Isaiah and Abby Cramer

ACTIVITY 1: *Understanding the Chapter (A Reading)*

1. The controlling factor that holds the diverse elements of Numbers 1–10 together is the symbolic significance of the _____ setting.

2. The purpose of the _____ in Numbers 1 is to enumerate the men eligible for _____ service for the invasion of the promised land.

3. Why did the census of Numbers 1 exclude the Levites?
   a) their ancestors Levi and Simeon had slaughtered the men of Shechem
   b) they had been selected to serve in the tabernacle
   c) their bloody zeal after the incident with the golden calf placed them under judgment
   d) the Levite rebellion in Leviticus included their abandonment of the wilderness sojourn

4. The large size of the tribe of _____ may reflect Genesis-shaped blessing since the Creator grants life by opening every womb. They also march _____ because of the blessing in Genesis.

5. Within the tribe of _____, Aaron's family are the priests. Yahweh takes the _____ permanently in place of the firstborn males who belonged to God based on _____ the firstborn of Egypt at the first Passover (Num 8:14–18). Yahweh turns around and gives them as a gift to _____ and his family (8:19). The line of _____ from this tribe is selected to carry the holy sanctuary furnishings through the wilderness (4:15). This may help explain the resentment that led to the rebellion of _____ and others (16:1–11).

6. Numbers 5 and 6 begin the pattern of the book routinely punctuated by new legal regulations to emphasize purity and _____. The _____ vow is a temporary vow for male or female individuals that involves abstaining from _____, fermented drinks, and touching corpses. The similarity to the town name _____, though unrelated, has led to pictures of _____ with long hair.

7. What element in Numbers 1–10 is not in chronological sequence?

    a) the priestly blessing (Num 6:24–26)

    b) dedication of the tabernacle (Num 7)

    c) cloud leading Israel (Num 9:15–17)

    d) blowing the silver trumpets (Num 10:1–8)

ACTIVITY 2: *Arranging the Camp (A Reading)*

The purpose of the first part of this activity is to recognize the **Genesis-shaped** and **Exodus-shaped** undercurrents in the tribal affiliations even concerning the wilderness camp arrangement around the tabernacle.

1. Read Numbers 2:3 and place the appropriate tribal name on the correct blank line of the diagram.

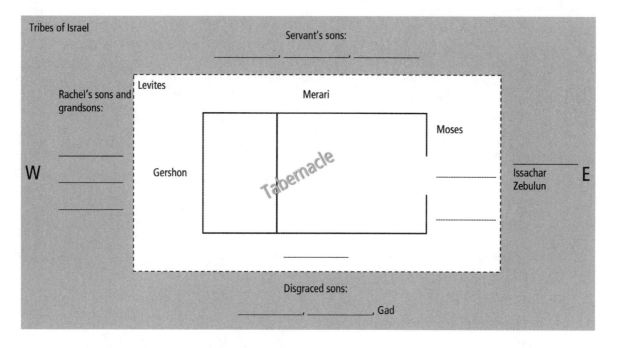

2. Read Genesis 43:8–10; 44:14; 46:28; 49:8–12. The tribe of _____ marches first (Num 2:9), camps first in front of the tabernacle (2:3), and worships first (7:12) according to their ancestor becoming a _____ and getting the blessing in Genesis (1 Chr 5:1–2).

3. Read Numbers 2:10–16 and place the appropriate tribal names on the correct blank lines of the diagram above.

4. Who disgraced himself with his stepmother (Gen 35:22; 49:3–4)? _____ Who murdered the men of Shechem (34:25–31; 49:5–7)? _____ and _____ Which tribe used their deadly zeal to bring God's judgment upon the idolaters at the mountain (Exod 32:25–29), thus moving from disgraced to ordained of God? _____

5. Read Numbers 2:18–24 and place the appropriate tribal names on the correct blank lines of the diagram above.

6. Who are Rachel's sons (Gen 30:22–23; 35:16–21)? _____ and _____ What did Joseph get that led to two tribes instead of one (1 Chr 5:1–2)? _____ Why does Joseph's younger son get ranked above his older son (Gen 48:17–20)? Jacob _____ him.

7. Read Numbers 2:25–31 and place the appropriate tribal names on the correct blank lines of the diagram above.

8. Who is the mother of the first tribal head (Gen 30:3–6)? _____ Who is the mother of the second tribal head (30:12)? _____ Who is the mother of the third tribal head (30:7–8)? _____

9. Read Numbers 3:38–39 and place the appropriate family names from the tribe of Levi on the correct blank lines of the diagram above.

10. Why does this person and his family camp in front of the tabernacle beside the family of Moses (Exod 28:1; Lev 8:1–13, 30)? They were ordained as _____. Which tribe camps around the tabernacle (Num 1:51–54)? _____

11. Read Numbers 3:27–32 and place the appropriate family name from the tribe of Levi on the correct blank line of the diagram above.

12. Why did a family line of the Levites get placed on the same side of the tabernacle where the disgraced tribes were encamped (Num 16:4; 26:5–10)? _____ and associates rebelled against Yahweh.

The purpose of the second part of the activity is to recognize the **Leviticus-shaped** effects of the new location of the tabernacle in relation to the wilderness camp.

13. Another name for the tabernacle is tent of _____ (Exod 40:34). At first the tabernacle was located _____ the camp (33:7). The tabernacle was relocated into the _____ of the camp (Num 2:17). The new location of the tabernacle caused some people to move _____ of the camp (5:1–4), namely, those with strong ritual impurities, such as those with _____ _____ (Lev 13:45–46), contact with a _____ (Num 19:11–13), and males and females with a _____ (Lev 15:2, 25). The new location of the tabernacle made it necessary for the _____ to protect the tribes of Israel from coming too _____ to the tabernacle (Num 1:51–54; 8:19).

ACTIVITY 3: *Making It Our Own (Another Look)*

1. Read Numbers 8:19. What did the Levites need to do to assist with the burden of holiness?

2. What are five key terms in Numbers 6:24–26 that embody Yahweh's mercy for his people?

22 TWO GENERATIONS IN THE WILDERNESS
(Numbers 10:11–21:35)

Isaiah and Abby Cramer

ACTIVITY 1: *Understanding the Chapter (A Reading)*

1. What is the major theme of Numbers 10–21, presented in a threefold repetition?

   a) success of the leaders and the people

   b) failures of the leaders and the people

   c) trials of the leaders and the people

   d) faithfulness of the leaders and failures of the people

2. The _____ embedded into Numbers 15 and 18–19 effectively divide the older (Num 10–14) and younger generations (20–21) with the (almost) thirty-eight _____ years in between (16–17).

3. In the first reading the younger generation sounds so much like their parents' generation that only the dating of Aaron's _____ later in Numbers indicates that the narrative has shifted to the next generation in Numbers 20.

4. What does Numbers 10–21 demonstrate about the younger wilderness generation?

   a) they are like the older generation

   b) they are different than the older generation

   c) they are more faithful than the older generation

   d) they are better prepared than the older generation

5. Moses is different from other _____ (Num 12:7). They see _____, but with Moses Yahweh speaks _____ to _____. (Fill in blanks with literal wording using Num 12:8 in the ESV; see BibleGateway.com if needed.) Elsewhere Moses speaks with Yahweh _____ to _____ as a person speaks to a friend (Exod 33:11). Yahweh would speak to Moses from between the _____ on the ark (Num 7:89).

6. How many scouts were sent into the land of promise? (select one)

   a) 40

   b) 21 (3 sets of 7)

   c) 12

   d) 7

7. How did the second report of the ten scouts re-present their findings?

    a) fictional distortion

    b) filled in the blanks with additional facts

    c) less detailed

    d) encouragement toward success

8. The only two persons of the older generation to go into the land of promise are _____ of the tribe of Judah and Joshua of the tribe of _____.

9. What is the half-truth in the rebellion of Korah, Dathan, Abiram, and On in Numbers 16:3?

    a) Aaron had gone too far with the golden calf

    b) Moses had gone too far with wearing the veil after he was with Yahweh

    c) leftover manna tasted bad

    d) Israel is called to be holy

10. Looking back later, who did the fiery snake "lifted up" on a pole prefigure?

    a) Messiah

    b) the serpent that was crushed

    c) the satan

    d) the seraphim (fiery ones of the celestial court of Isa 6:2)

ACTIVITY 2: *Grumbling, Grumbling, Grumbling (A Reading)*

1. Fill in the chart. Only the reference of the complaint is provided. Study the entire context to locate the answers.

Numbers	Complainer(s)	Complaint	Moses's reaction	God's reaction
11:1	Israel	hardships	prays	fire
11:4–6				(two actions) Spirit on seventy elders and quails for the people
12:1–2	(two persons)			
14:2–4				

Numbers	Complainer(s)	Complaint	Moses's reaction	God's reaction
16:3, 12–14	(four persons)			(three actions) affirms choice of Aaron; fire to consume the 250; earth swallows up families of Korah and associates
16:41				
20:2–5				
21:5				(initial and second actions)

2. Using the chart above, fill in the pie chart on the left according to approximate percentages/proportions relative to what the leaders and the people grumbled about in the wilderness. The largest piece is done for you as well as all Scripture references.

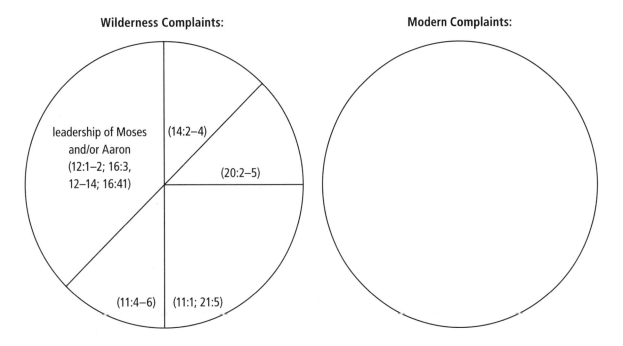

3. Spend a few minutes thinking through the sorts of things modern Christians grumble about. Divide up the pie chart on the right (no more than eight pieces) according to approximate percentages/proportions relative to modern Christian complaints. Label each piece.

ACTIVITY 3: *Learning from Wilderness Rebellions (Psalm 106)*

Later biblical writers frequently interpret older Scriptures when teaching and challenging their own constituents. The purpose of this activity is to think through the psalmist's interpretation of selected elements in Numbers.

1. Place the following Scripture references in the appropriate blanks that appear immediately after the elements to which the references allude: • Num 11:4; • Num 11:33–34; • Num 14:22; • Num 16:3, 13–14; • Num 16:26, 35; • Deut 11:6.

   ¹³But they soon forgot what he had done and did not wait for his plan to unfold. ¹⁴In the desert they gave in to their craving [_____]; in the wilderness they put God to the test [_____]. ¹⁵So he gave them what they asked for, but sent a wasting disease among them [_____]. ¹⁶In the camp they grew envious of Moses and of Aaron [_____], who was consecrated to Yahweh. ¹⁷The earth opened up and swallowed Dathan; it buried the company of Abiram [_____]. ¹⁸Fire blazed among their followers; a flame consumed the wicked [_____]. (Ps 106:13–18)

2. What is the underlying problem the psalmist identifies that led to these many rebellions in the wilderness?

3. Place the following Scripture references in the appropriate blanks that appear immediately after the elements to which the references allude: Num 14:29, 32; Deut 1:27; Deut 1:32; Ezek 20:23.

   ²⁴Then they despised the pleasant land; they did not believe [_____] his promise. ²⁵They grumbled in their tents [_____] and did not obey Yahweh. ²⁶So he swore to them with uplifted hand that he would make them fall in the wilderness [_____], ²⁷make their descendants fall among the nations and scatter them throughout the lands [_____]. (Ps 106:24–27)

4. What did Israel privately claim about Yahweh that led to their unbelief (Deut 1:27, 32)?

5. Place the following Scripture references in the appropriate blanks that appear immediately after the elements to which the references allude: Num 27:14; Deut 1:37; Deut 3:26; Deut 4:21; Deut 32:51 (Deut 32:51 needs to be used in two blanks).

> They provoked him to anger by the waters of Meribah [**Num 20:13** and _____], so Moses claimed that it went badly for Moses because of them [_____ and _____ and _____], for they made his spirit bitter, and he spoke rashly with his own mouth [**Num 20:12** and _____ and _____]. (Ps 106:32–33 lit.)

6. Does the psalmist acknowledge Moses's repeated claim against the people (Deut 1:37; 3:26; 4:21)? (choose one) Yes or No

7. What are the claims of the narrators of Numbers and Deuteronomy that the psalmist interprets as Moses's rash talk by his own mouth (Num 20:12; 27:14; Deut 32:51)?

ACTIVITY 4: *Making It Our Own (Another Look)*

1. Read Numbers 11:4–6; 14:2–3; 16:12–13. What were the underlying motives that led to the distorted fictions the rebels used to excuse themselves?

2. Compare and contrast Deuteronomy 1:27 and 4:37–38 in terms of looking forward versus looking backward and the viewpoint on Yahweh's relationship with his people. Why are these two views of the same realities so different?

23 THE SECOND GENERATION ON THE PLAINS OF MOAB
(Numbers 22–36)

ACTIVITY 1: *Understanding the Chapter (A Reading)*

Draw a line connecting the passage with its contents.

1. Numbers 22–24		offerings and vows
2. Numbers 25		Balaam narratives
3. Numbers 26		Zelophehad's daughters
4. Numbers 27:1–11		military census of second generation
5. Numbers 27:12–23		fornication and idolatry with other women
6. Numbers 28–30		appointing Moses's replacement

Draw a line connecting the passage with its contents.

7. Numbers 31		rebellion and settlement of Transjordan tribes
8. Numbers 32		apportioning the land
9. Numbers 33		travel itinerary through the wilderness
10. Numbers 34		Zelophehad's daughters
11. Numbers 35		battle report against Midian
12. Numbers 36		cities of Levites and of refuge

13. What is the name of the Moabite king who hired a prophet to curse Israel? _____

14. What is the name of the wicked person who concocted a conspiracy with the Moabites and Midianites to tempt the Israelites into polytheistic lust and debauchery? _____

15. What is the name of the person who delivered Israel from the conspiracy of the Moabites and Midianites? _____

16. Which tribe was the largest in the census of the second generation of Israelites? _____

17. What is the name of the two and a half Transjordan tribes who already had received their land inheritance by the conquests that Moses led against the Transjordan kingdoms of Sihon and Og? _____, _____, and the half tribe of _____

18. Who died without leaving any male heirs? _____

19. According to Numbers 30, what is the social status of a female who did **not** need to get permission from a male in her immediate family in order to make a vow? _____ (30:__)

20. According to Numbers 33, how many places did Israel camp after leaving Egypt and arriving at the Jordan River? _____

ACTIVITY 2: *Balaam's Oracles (A Reading)*

1. Underline the verbal parallels between the blessing of Judah and the third oracle of Balaam. Also underline the similar imagery in Balaam's second oracle.

2. Use broken underlining to mark similar language in the blessings of Abraham and Jacob and Balaam's third oracle.

3. Use wavy underlining to mark additional similar language in Balaam's second and third oracles.

Promises to Hebrew Ancestors

[to Abraham] I will bless those who bless you,
    and whoever curses you I will curse;
and all peoples on earth
    will be blessed through you. (Gen 12:3)

[to Jacob] May nations serve you
    and peoples bow down to you.
Be lord over your brothers,
    and may the sons of your mother bow down to you.
May those who curse you be cursed
    and those who bless you be blessed. (Gen 27:29)

You are a lion's cub, Judah;
    you return from the prey, my son.
Like a lion he crouches and lies down,
    like a lioness—who dares to rouse him? (Gen 49:9)

Balaam's Second Oracle	Balaam's Third Oracle

<table>
<tr><td>

²¹No misfortune is seen in Jacob,

    no misery observed in Israel.

Yahweh their God is with them;

    the shout of the King is among them.

²²God brought them out of Egypt;

    they have the strength of a wild ox.

²³There is no divination against Jacob,

    no evil omens against Israel.

It will now be said of Jacob

    and of Israel, "See what God has done!"

²⁴The people rise like a lioness;

    they rouse themselves like a lion

that does not rest till it devours its prey

    and drinks the blood of its victims. (Num 23:21–24)

</td><td>

⁷Water will flow from his buckets;

    his seed will have abundant water.

"His king will be greater than Agag;

    his kingdom will be exalted.

⁸God brought him out of Egypt;

    like the strength of a wild ox for him.

He devours hostile nations and breaks their

    bones in pieces;

    his arrows pierce them.

⁹Like a lion they crouch and lie down,

    like a lioness—who dares to rouse him?

May those who bless you be blessed

    and those who curse you be cursed!

    (Num 24:7–9 lit.)

</td></tr>
</table>

4. Based on the interpretive blending of the blessings of Abraham, Jacob, and Judah in the third oracle, does Balaam regard the expected Judah-king to fulfill the Abrahamic covenant? (choose one) Yes or No

5. Does the shift of pronoun from third person plural (them) in Balaam's second oracle to third person singular (him) in the third oracle relate to the expectations for the king? (choose one) Yes or No

6. Compare the similar imagery of what Yahweh accomplished in Balaam's second oracle and what he will accomplish in the third oracle. How does Balaam's third oracle anticipate the development of the expectation for a new exodus?

The next set of comparisons needs due caution because of the textual issue in Numbers 24:17 (see footnote below).

7. Mark with <u>underlining</u> the shared language between the blessing of Judah and Balaam's fourth oracle.

8. Mark with <u>broken underlining</u> the similar imagery in the curse of the serpent and Balaam's fourth oracle.

> And I will put enmity
>> between you and the woman,
>> and between your offspring and hers;
> he will crush your head,
>> and you will strike his heel. (Gen 3:15)

> The scepter will not depart from Judah,
>> nor the ruler's staff from between his feet,
> until he to whom it belongs shall come
>> and the obedience of the nations shall be his. (Gen 49:10)

> [Balaam's fourth oracle] I see him, but not now;
>> I behold him, but not near.
> A star will come out of Jacob;
>> a scepter will rise out of Israel.
> He will crush the foreheads of Moab,
>> the skulls of all the people of Sheth. (Num 24:17)*

9. How does Balaam (possible—see footnote) advance imagery from the curse upon the serpent and the Judah-king in the expectation of the star of Jacob?

10. <u>Underline</u> the shared imagery of the ancient poets and Jeremiah.

11. Use <u>broken underlining</u> to mark the shared imagery between Balaam and Jeremiah.

---

* The Hebrew term in Numbers 24:17 might be "foreheads" as in NIV here and NRSVue and most modern committee versions or "borderlands" as in the text note of NRSVue (see BibleGateway.com). If Balaam does not use the smashing heads of Moab imagery first, then Jeremiah does later (see Jer 48:45 below). For an evaluation of the evidence of this textual difficulty see Gary Edward Schnittjer, "The Blessing of Judah as Generative Expectation," *Bibliotheca Sacra* 177 (2020): 23–24.

12. Circle the verb the poets used of Chemosh's children. Circle the verb that Jeremiah used concerning the children of Chemosh.

[The poets say:] ²⁸Fire went out from Heshbon, a blaze from the city of Sihon. It consumed Ar of Moab, the citizens of Arnon's heights. ²⁹Woe to you, Moab! You are destroyed, people of Chemosh! He has given up his sons as fugitives and his daughters as captives to Sihon king of the Amorites. (Num 21:28–29)

⁴⁵In the shadow of Heshbon the fugitives stand helpless, for a fire has gone out from Heshbon, a blaze from the midst of Sihon; it consumes the foreheads of Moab, and the skulls of the noisy boasters. ⁴⁶Woe to you, Moab! The people of Chemosh are destroyed; your sons are taken captive and your daughters into captivity. (Jer 48:45–46 lit.)

[Balaam says:] I see him but not now, I behold him but not near, a star will come out from Jacob, and a scepter will rise from Israel, and it will crush the foreheads of Moab, and the skulls of all the people of Sheth. (Num 24:17 lit.)

13. Elsewhere Jeremiah frequently recycles prophetic oracles of Israel's prophets like Isaiah. Jeremiah 48:45–46 is remarkable because Jeremiah repackages and combines oracles from non-Israelite prophetic outsiders embedded in Numbers—ancient poets and Balaam. The ancient poets had given credit to Moab's patron deity Chemosh for their downfall (see Num 21:29). Read Deuteronomy 2:9. How does Jeremiah "correct" the ancient poet's theology so it agrees with the outlook in Deuteronomy promoting Yahweh's sovereignty (see circled items above)?

ACTIVITY 3: *Wilderness Geography (A Reading)*

For help with geography activities, the best option is a biblical atlas from a library. In addition, many Bibles have maps near the back, or you can use the maps in *Torah Story*.

Exodus and Numbers only narrate three journeys and three encampments (see *Torah Story*, Table 20-D, p. 324). This is greatly streamlined for narrative purposes as compared with the more detailed travel itinerary of forty encampments listed in Numbers 33 (see *Torah Story*, Table 23-G, p. 375).

1. Place the following labels on the correct lines: • Edom, • Jericho, • Kadesh Barnea, • plains of Moab, • Sinai (traditional location).

2. Read Numbers 10:12 and 12:16 and draw an arrow of this stage of Israel's journey.

3. Read Numbers 20:18–21 and draw an arrow that goes around this entire region to the south, then east, then finally toward their arrival in the place mentioned in Numbers 22:1.

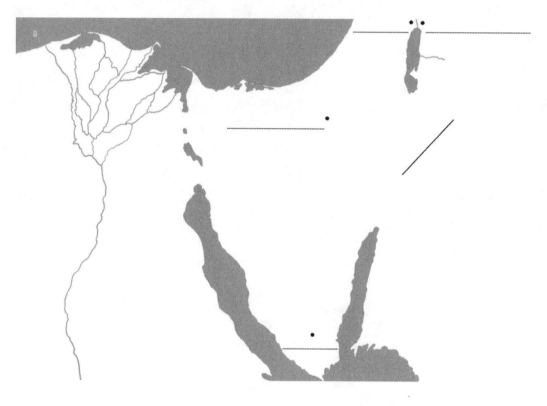

4. Read Numbers 21:21–25, 31, 33–35; Deut 2:8–9. On the map below place the following names of regions and their kings in parentheses on the appropriate tilted lines as well as the city next to its dot:
• BASHAN (Og); • AMORITES (Sihon); • MOAB; • Jericho.

5. Read Numbers 32:33–42. On the map below place the names of the two and half tribes that inherited the land of the Transjordan on their lines.

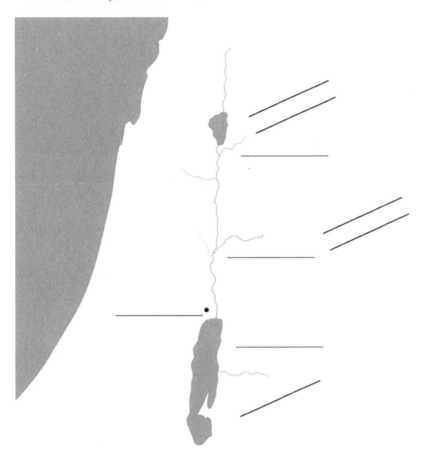

ACTIVITY 4: *Making It Our Own (Another Look)*

1. Read Numbers 27:1–11. Why did Zelophehad die? How did Yahweh respond to the request of the daughters?

2. Read Numbers 36:1–13. What is the complaint of the families of Manasseh? How does Yahweh respond to their complaint?

3. Read Numbers 9:1–14. What is the complaint of the group of ritually impure persons? How does Yahweh respond to their complaint?

4. Do the rulings of Yahweh in the preceding three legal cases suggest that the purpose of the law is to demand compliance, or is their purpose relational? (Provide evidence from these biblical contexts, including Scripture references, to support your answer.)

21 MACROVIEW OF DEUTERONOMY

ACTIVITY 1: *Understanding the Chapter (A Reading)*

Match heading and chapters

1. ___ Deuteronomy 1–4

2. ___ Deuteronomy 4:44–28:68

3. ___ Deuteronomy 29–30

4. ___ Deuteronomy 33

A This is the torah

B This is the blessing

C These are the words

D These are the words of the covenant

5. What is the relationship between obedience and love of God in Deuteronomy?

    a) obey the law in order to love God

    b) love God in order to obey the law

    c) to love God means there is no need for obedience

    d) obedience of law, not love of God, is the only requirement in the Old Testament

6. What sort of second-person pronouns does Deuteronomy use?

    a) always singular because of a focus on individual faith

    b) always plural because individual faith is only important in the New Testament

    c) mixture of singular and plural emphasizing individual responsibility and collective identity

    d) neither since ancient Hebrews considered second-person direct address offensive

7. Who speaks in Deuteronomy? (choose all that apply)

    a) Yahweh

    b) Moses

    c) Aaron

    d) the narrator

ACTIVITY 2: *"You" (A Reading)*

Deuteronomy 5 re-presents the ten words revealed at the mountain in Exodus 20 forty years earlier to the older generation who had all died in the wilderness. Below an ultra-literal translation of Deuteronomy 5:3 is provided for the next few questions. The commas in this translation follow the disjunctive pauses according to the medieval Judaic secretaries known as Masoretes. Moses says:

> Not with our ancestors did Yahweh cut this covenant [ten words],
>> but with us,
>> us,
>> those here today,
>> all of us alive. (Deut 5:3 lit.)

1. According to Moses in Deuteronomy 5:3, who were **not** the recipients of the ten words? ____ _____

2. How many times does Moses identify his immediate listening constituents in Deuteronomy as the original recipients of the ten words in Deuteronomy 5:3? _____

3. What is the narrator's view of Moses's mental prowess (Deut 34:7)?
   a) since Moses is over one hundred years old he sometimes confused older and younger generations
   b) Moses could not see the people before him because of wearing a veil to hide the glory
   c) Moses had endured so much immediate revelation that his perceptions were distorted
   d) Moses is mentally and visually vigorous

4. Why does Moses so strongly emphasize the covenant symbolized by the ten words as directly owned by the present generation before him in Deuteronomy 5:3?
   a) it is nothing more than vivid language
   b) he erases any place for the next generation to shirk responsibility to the covenant
   c) he knew that salvation by works required strenuous effort
   d) he did not need to understand what he was saying since he was taking dictation from the Holy Spirit

5. First-person discourse means to speak of oneself (I, me, we, us), second person to directly address another (you), and third person to talk about another (she, he, it, they, them, their). Underline all of the second-person pronouns in Deuteronomy 30:1–5.

> ¹When all these blessings and curses I have set before you come on you and you take them to heart wherever Yahweh your God disperses you among the nations, ²and when you and your children return to Yahweh your God and obey him with all your heart and with all your soul according to everything I command you today, ³then Yahweh your God will restore your fortunes and have compassion on you and gather you again from all the nations where he scattered you. ⁴Even if you have been banished to the most distant land under the heavens, from there Yahweh your God will gather you and bring you back. ⁵He will bring you to the land that belonged to your ancestors, and you will take possession of it. He will make you more prosperous and numerous than your ancestors. (Deut 30:1–5)

Answer the next few questions using Deuteronomy 30:1–5 that you marked above and this basic timeline (on earlier and later date of the exodus see *Torah Story*, Sidebar 13-B in Chapter 13).

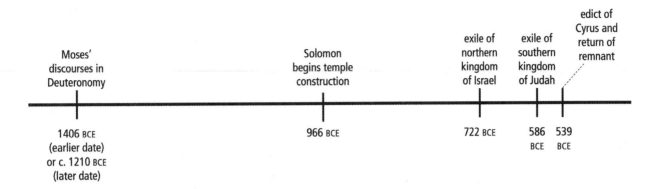

6. What date corresponds to the first "you" in Deuteronomy 30:1 based on the earlier date? _____ BCE
And based on the later date? _____ BCE

7. Remember BCE dates count down (subtract the lower number from the higher number to discover the number of years between the two dates). Approximately how many years after the earlier date of Moses's discourses is the last "you" set in Deuteronomy 30:1 if referring to the exile of Judah? _____ years
And based on the later date? _____ years

8. Remember BCE dates count down (subtract the lower number from the higher number to discover the number of years between the two dates). Approximately how many years after the earlier date of Moses's discourses is the last "you" set in Deuteronomy 30:4? _____ years
And based on the later date? _____ years

9. In what year is the first "you" of Deuteronomy 30:5 set? _____ BCE

10. Who are the "ancestors" referred to in Deuteronomy 30:5?
a) Abraham, Isaac, and Jacob
b) Abraham and Sarah
c) the congregation standing before Moses
d) the exilic parents of the returning remnant

11. What is the significance of the elastic shared collective identity of "you"—the second-person addressees—in Deuteronomy?

ACTIVITY 3: *Making It Our Own (Another Look)*

1. Study Deuteronomy 30:6. Why is it inadequate to reduce the theology of Deuteronomy to "obedience brings blessing and disobedience brings cursing," as is done so often?

2. In Deuteronomy 30:6, what comes before loving Yahweh your God—the basis of any real obedience?

3. Who is the subject of the first verb in Deuteronomy 30:6? _____
How does this bear on loving Yahweh and covenantal faithfulness by his people?

ACTIVITY 1: *Understanding the Chapter (A Reading)*

1. Deuteronomy is set on the plains of _____ across the _____ River from Jericho. The congregation of Israel stood on a threshold, as it were, with the _____ in their past and the land of promise in their future.

2. What is the name of Mount Sinai in Deuteronomy? Mount _____

For help with geography activities, the best option is a biblical atlas from a library. In addition, many Bibles have maps near the back, or you can use the maps in *Torah Story*.

3. Read Deuteronomy 1:1–5. Fill in the correct blanks on the map below with the following places: Horeb, Jericho, Kadesh Barnea, plains of Moab, and Mount Seir.

4. Based on Deuteronomy 1:1–5, fill in the correct times in the appropriate blanks on the map below.

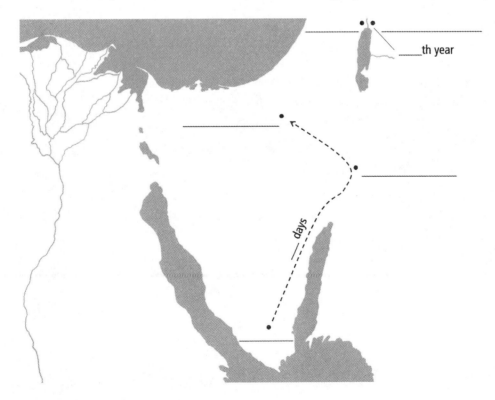

5. The majority of the persons in the congregation of Israel standing before Moses in Deuteronomy had no personal knowledge of _____, for they had grown up in the wilderness.

Match (answers may be used more than once or not at all)

6. ___ Selection of seventy elders   **A** Exodus 18 only

7. ___ Miriam contracts skin disease   **B** Numbers 11

8. ___ Moses complained to God   **C** Deuteronomy 1:9–18 only

9. ___ Moses complained to father-in-law   **D** Exodus 18 and Deuteronomy 1:9–18

10. ___ Moses complained to the people   **E** None of the above

11. ___ Set at Mount Sinai (implied)

12. ___ Judges appointed over thousands, hundreds, fifties, tens

13. ___ Moses warns the judges against showing partiality

14. For who else besides Israel had Yahweh driven out others so that they could inherit their land?
    a) Philistines
    b) Phoenicians
    c) Assyrians and Neo-Babylonians
    d) Ammonites and Edomites

15. Who else besides Israel defeated large-sized others comparable to the Anakites?
    a) Philistines and Phoenicians
    b) Assyrians
    c) Neo-Babylonians
    d) Ammonites and Moabites

16. What Israelites does the biblical text credit with defeating giant people?
    a) Abraham, Jacob, Caleb, and David and their associates
    b) Moses, Joshua, Caleb, and David and their associates
    c) Judah, Ephraim, Joshua, and David and their associates
    d) Noah, Nimrod, Moses, and David and their associates

17. In what sense did the congregation before Moses in Deuteronomy see and hear the signs against Egypt and the revelation at the mountain?

ACTIVITY 2: *Kadesh Rebellion Revisited (Deuteronomy 1:19–45)*

Compare the story of the rebellion at Kadesh in Numbers 13–14 and Deuteronomy 1:19–45. In the following table list the appropriate verse references from either or both accounts and mark lack of reference by two hyphens (--). A few have been done for you as examples.

	Numbers	Deuteronomy
1. People desire to send scouts		
2. Yahweh affirms decision to send scouts		
Scouting expedition	13:4–24	1:24–25a
3. Official report of the scouts		
4. Caleb's recommendation of invasion		
5. Second bad report of scouts in public		
6. Reminiscences of second bad report in private		
7. Israel's collective revolt in public		
8. Moses and Aaron fall on faces		
9. Advice not to fear from Caleb and Joshua		
10. Advice not to fear from Moses		
Moses intercedes before Yahweh	14:11–19	--
Judgment of older generation	14:20–32, 34–35	1:34–38
11. Younger generation spared		
Remain in wilderness	14:34–35	1:40
Plague against ten scouts	14:36–38	--
The people's ill-advised invasion	14:39–45	1:41–46

12. Carefully study the public and private rebellions of the people in numbers 6 and 7 above. What is the basic public accusation against Yahweh (with Scripture references), and what is the basic private accusation against Yahweh (with Scripture references)?

ACTIVITY 3: *Blame Game (Another Look)*

This activity deals with whose fault it is that Moses cannot go into the land of promise. Circle correct answers from choices in the parentheses.

1. According to Numbers 20:12 it is the fault of (choose one) Moses or the people as explained by (choose one) the narrator or direct speech of Yahweh.

2. According to Numbers 27:14 it is the fault of (choose one) Moses or the people as explained by (choose one) the narrator or direct speech of Yahweh.

3. According to Deuteronomy 1:37 it is the fault of (choose one) Moses or the people as explained by (choose one) the narrator or direct speech of Moses.

4. According to Deuteronomy 3:26 it is the fault of (choose one) Moses or the people as explained by (choose one) the narrator or direct speech of Moses.

5. According to Deuteronomy 4:21–22 it is the fault of (choose one) Moses or the people as explained by (choose one) the narrator or direct speech of Moses.

6. According to Deuteronomy 32:51 it is the fault of (choose one) Moses or the people as explained by (choose one) the narrator or direct speech of Yahweh.

7. Why is it so difficult for people to confess their sinfulness, since even Moses struggles to admit his own blameworthiness for his sin?

ACTIVITY 4: *Making It Our Own (Deuteronomy 4)*

Matching. Look up the passages and determine the event to which each looks back.

1. ___ Deuteronomy 4:10–12, 15   **A** creation

2. ___ Deuteronomy 4:13   **B** deliverance from Egypt

3. ___ Deuteronomy 4:32   **C** Ten Commandments

4. ___ Deuteronomy 4:33   **D** revelation at the mountain

5. ___ Deuteronomy 4:34–35   **E** defeat of the Transjordanian kingdoms

6. ___ Deuteronomy 4:36

7. ___ Deuteronomy 4:37

8. ___ Deuteronomy 4:38

9. ___ Deuteronomy 5:6–21

10. Deuteronomy 4 includes thirteen verses looking back to what Yahweh has done (verses 10–12, 13, 14, 15, 32, 33, 34–35, 36, 37, 38) and twenty-three verses offering motivation to the congregation of Israel before Moses (verses 5–9, 16–31, 39–40) (see Table 25-B in Chapter 25). Carefully study Deuteronomy 4, paying attention to the relationship of looking back to what Yahweh has done and the motivations built into the passage. How does looking back at what Yahweh has done help his people who need to be motivated to serve him in the challenges ahead?

26 THE TEN WORDS AND THE COMMAND
(Deuteronomy 4:44–11:32)

iStock.com/Algul

ACTIVITY 1: *Understanding the Chapter (A Reading)*

1. According to Moses in Deuteronomy 5:3–4, who are the recipients of the covenant represented by the ten words?

   a) the Hebrew ancestors in Genesis

   b) the older generation forty years earlier

   c) the present generation

   d) exclusively Moses himself since he alone went up the mountain

2. The covenantal relationship between Yahweh and his people extends to each generation as represented in the _____ of the covenant in Deuteronomy 5, Joshua 5, and Joshua 24.

3. Which version of the fourth commandment to honor the Sabbath is based on the pattern established on the seventh day by the Creator?

   a) Exodus 20

   b) Deuteronomy 5

   c) both Exodus 20 and Deuteronomy 5

   d) neither Exodus 20 nor Deuteronomy 5

4. Which version of the fourth commandment to honor the Sabbath extending to all within a household is based on the redemption of the people from Egyptian bondage?

   a) Exodus 20

   b) Deuteronomy 5

   c) both Exodus 20 and Deuteronomy 5

   d) neither Exodus 20 nor Deuteronomy 5

5. Which version of the tenth commandment prohibiting coveting sets off not coveting a neighbor's spouse separately from the rest of the list?

   a) Exodus 20

   b) Deuteronomy 5

   c) both Exodus 20 and Deuteronomy 5

   d) neither Exodus 20 nor Deuteronomy 5

For questions 6 and 7, the Hebrew of Deuteronomy 6:4 says:

"Hear! O Israel, Yahweh our God Yahweh one/only." (lit)

6. Which translation of Deuteronomy 6:4–5a emphasizes Yahweh himself as the basis for loving God in 6:5a?

    a) Hear, O Israel: Yahweh our God, Yahweh is one. Love Yahweh. (NIV*)

    b) Hear, O Israel: Yahweh is our God, Yahweh alone. You shall love Yahweh. (NRSVue*)

    c) both NIV and NRSVue

    d) neither NIV nor NRSVue

7. Which translation of Deuteronomy 6:4–5a emphasizes Israel's loyalty as the basis for loving God in 6:5a?

    a) Hear, O Israel: Yahweh our God, Yahweh is one. Love Yahweh. (NIV*)

    b) Hear, O Israel: Yahweh is our God, Yahweh alone. You shall love Yahweh. (NRSVue*)

    c) both NIV and NRSVue

    d) neither NIV nor NRSVue

8. In what sense is the great command creational?

    a) because the full "Hear, O Israel" proclamation is seven words long in Hebrew like the days of creation

    b) because the great command can only be fulfilled in Eden

    c) because we are made in God's image, we are designed to love him

    d) because the great command was issued in a formless and void wilderness environment

9. What Scriptures did Messiah quote in the face of his three temptations?

    a) from all over Deuteronomy

    b) three from Deuteronomy 6–11

    c) one from each of the five books of Torah

    d) he only quoted from Psalms to avoid legalism by following Torah

10. The threefold "you may say to yourselves" in Deuteronomy 7:17; 8:17; and 9:4 underscores three _____, namely, military might, prosperity, and self-righteousness. The problem is not with the gifts themselves but that the people forget the _____.

---

* NIV and NRSVue have been modified with "Yahweh" instead of "the Lord."

ACTIVITY 2: *Youthful Questions (A Reading, Deuteronomy 6:20–25)*

1. <u>Underline</u> the question of the younger generation in the excerpts from Exodus 13 and Deuteronomy 6.

> [11]After Yahweh brings you into the land of the Canaanites and gives it to you, as he promised on oath to you and your ancestors, [12]you are to give over to Yahweh the first offspring of every womb. All the firstborn males of your livestock belong to Yahweh. [13]Redeem with a lamb every firstborn donkey, but if you do not redeem it, break its neck. Redeem every firstborn among your sons. [14]In days to come, when your son asks you, "What does this mean?" say to him, "With a mighty hand Yahweh brought us out of Egypt, out of the land of slavery. [15]When Pharaoh stubbornly refused to let us go, Yahweh killed the firstborn of both people and animals in Egypt. This is why I sacrifice to Yahweh the first male offspring of every womb and redeem each of my firstborn sons." [16]And it will be like a sign on your hand and a symbol on your forehead that Yahweh brought us out of Egypt with his mighty hand. (Exod 13:11–16)

> [20]In the future, when your son asks you, "What is the meaning of the stipulations, decrees and laws Yahweh our God has commanded you?" [21]tell him: "We were slaves of Pharaoh in Egypt, but Yahweh brought us out of Egypt with a mighty hand. [22]Before our eyes Yahweh sent signs and wonders—great and terrible—on Egypt and Pharaoh and his whole household. [23]But he brought us out from there to bring us in and give us the land he promised on oath to our ancestors. [24]Yahweh commanded us to obey all these decrees and to fear Yahweh our God, so that we might always prosper and be kept alive, as is the case today. [25]And if we are careful to obey all this law before Yahweh our God, as he has commanded us, that will be our righteousness." (Deut 6:20–25)

2. What is similar about the answers to the next generation in Exodus 13 and Deuteronomy 6 regarding the redemption of the firstborn of humans and animals and the reason for the laws from Yahweh?

3. In the answer of the older generation in Deuteronomy 6:21–25, which comes first? (choose one) redemption or command

4. Why is it important that the reason for Yahweh's commands in Deuteronomy 6:20–25 is in the form of a narrative?

ACTIVITY 3: *Banned Marriages (Deuteronomy 7:3–4)*

1. Read Exodus 34:16. If read literally and in isolation, this prohibition is (choose one) for only one gender or gender inclusive.

2. Deuteronomy 7:3 interpretively advances the prohibition against intermarriage so that it is explicitly (choose one) for only one gender or gender inclusive.

3. The restoration assembly is sometimes accused of being sexist for only sending away unbelieving wives of apostasy marriages (e.g., Ezra 10:44). What does the evidence in Ezra 9:12; Nehemiah 10:30; and 13:25 suggest about the restoration assembly's application of the legal prohibitions against apostasy marriages relative to gender?

4. The prohibitions against apostasy marriages in Exodus 34:16 and Deuteronomy 7:4 are based on (choose one) racial purity or danger of turning from Yahweh.

5. Read 2 Corinthians 6:14 and its context. What reasons do Paul and Timothy offer for their prohibition against apostasy marriages?

ACTIVITY 4: *(A Reading, Deuteronomy 8)*

1. Circle the uses of the terms "forget" and "remember" in Deuteronomy 8:11–20.

2. Underline the two related reasons why Israel might forget.

3. Use broken underlining to mark the dangers of forgetting.

> [11]Be careful that you do not forget Yahweh your God, failing to observe his commands, his laws and his decrees that I am giving you this day. [12]Otherwise, when you eat and are satisfied, when you build fine houses and settle down, [13]and when your herds and flocks grow large and your silver and gold increase and

all you have is multiplied, [14]then your heart will become proud and you will forget Yahweh your God, who brought you out of Egypt, out of the land of slavery. [15]He led you through the vast and dreadful wilderness, that thirsty and waterless land, with its venomous snakes and scorpions. He brought you water out of hard rock. [16]He gave you manna to eat in the wilderness, something your ancestors had never known, to humble and test you so that in the end it might go well with you. [17]You may say to yourself, "My power and the strength of my hands have produced this wealth for me." [18]But remember Yahweh your God, for it is he who gives you the ability to produce wealth, and so confirms his covenant, which he swore to your ancestors, as it is today. [19]If you ever forget Yahweh your God and follow other gods and worship and bow down to them, I testify against you today that you will surely be destroyed. [20]Like the nations Yahweh destroyed before you, so you will be destroyed for not obeying Yahweh your God. (Deut 8:11–20)

4. How does the warning in Deuteronomy 8 cause problems for those who claim Yahweh's covenant with Israel grants them privileges based on their ethnicity?

ACTIVITY 5: *Making It Our Own (Another Look)*

1. If Deuteronomy 6:6–9 addresses (choose one) older generation or younger generation, then the allusions to it in Proverbs 3:1–3; 6:20–22; and 7:1–3 present what they need to say to the (choose one) older generation or younger generation.

2. The term _____ in Deuteronomy 4:13; 5:22; 9:9–11, 15, 17; 10:1, 3 refers to that which the _____ words were written upon. What is the significance of using this somewhat rare term outside Torah in Proverbs 3:3 and 7:3?

3. In the warning to the younger generation in Proverbs 7, how are acts of religious devotion misused in 7:14?

27 THE RULES AND REGULATIONS
(Deuteronomy 12–28)

© 2018 Zondervan

ACTIVITY 1: *Understanding the Chapter (A Reading)*

1. The command to love God in Deuteronomy 6:4–9 serves as a basis for any true _____ of the rules and regulations of the torah collection of Deuteronomy 12–26.

2. While "the command" provides an exposition of the first word, in a broad sense what are the rules and regulations of the torah collection designed to provide?
   a) a list of various ways to apply the first word
   b) an exposition of the other words
   c) an evaluation of the forty years spent in the wilderness
   d) a test to demonstrate the reader's comprehension of the first word

3. How does the instruction for a central place of worship relate to monotheism?
   a) because Yahweh is one, his people were to be one
   b) because Yahweh is one, the place of worship had to be portable
   c) because Yahweh is one, the people could worship in any manner they saw fit
   d) because Yahweh is one, his shining glory could only be seen at one place at a time

4. Jeroboam set up worship centers at which two cities?
   a) Dan and Bethel
   b) Dan and Beersheba
   c) Bethlehem and Hebron
   d) Hebron and Jerusalem

5. In what ways does the Torah support the view that God intended Israel to have a human king of God's choosing?
   a) Moses's appointment of judges anticipated the need for monarchy
   b) the crown worn by the high priest gave implicit approval of monarchy
   c) Torah gives no support of a human king over Israel since only God is to be their king
   d) the blessing of Judah and Balaam's oracles looked for a coming king

6. The downfall of what Israelite king is told in such a way that it echoes the instructions concerning kings found in Deuteronomy?

    a) Rehoboam

    b) Solomon

    c) Jeroboam

    d) Uzziah

7. What reason does Moses give in Deuteronomy for the command to destroy the Canaanites?

    a) Israel's God racially discriminated against Canaanites

    b) to offer an example to other nations that did not obey

    c) Canaanites were incapable of conversion

    d) to prevent Israel from rebelling against God's word

8. The prohibition to exclude the Moabites from the assembly of Yahweh is based on (choose one) the racial inferiority of the Moabites or the Moabites' refusal of hospitality to Israel's needs in the wilderness.

9. What is the significance of the "third generation" concerning assimilation into the assembly of Yahweh in Deuteronomy 23?

    a) Israelites were to permit gentiles to enter when they turn three years old

    b) the third generation was traditionally devoted to Yahweh for service in the temple

    c) one's devotion to God's ways was demonstrated in the faith of one's grandchildren

    d) to be willing to sacrifice the second generation

10. When interpreting laws in Torah the best commentary on the Bible is the _____.

11. Understanding the laws requires an attitude akin to the psalmist that instructions are like treasures that need to be discovered and _____.

ACTIVITY 2: *Killing Canaanites (A Reading)*

1. List three commands, one each in Deuteronomy 7:2, 3, and 5.

    •

    •

    •

2. The reason for devoting the nations of Canaan in Deuteronomy 7:4 is (choose one) racial prejudice or to protect Israel from serving false gods.

3. Compare Exodus 34:11* and Deuteronomy 7:1–2. What does Deuteronomy 7:1–2 add to the legal standards for invading the land of promise not included in earlier versions of the law?

4. Read Numbers 21:1–3, which includes the first use of "devote" (lit.) in a military context in the Bible. The idea for devoting the peoples of Canaan is initiated by (choose one) Yahweh or Israel because of (choose one) racial hatred or a crisis. Since Yahweh fulfilled Israel's request to give over the peoples of Canaan (Num 21:3), he held Israel to their _____ and added "devote" the nations of Canaan to the legal standard for invasion of the land (Deut 7:2).

5. Read Deuteronomy 7:1. The law to devote the nations of Canaan is (choose one) for all places and all times or only applicable when Israel invades the land of promise.

6. Read Deuteronomy 7:4 and 20:18. The law to devote the nations of Canaan is based on (choose one) racist hatred or extreme protection of Israel from rebellion.

7. In Romans 9:6 Paul says, "not all who are descended from Israel are _____." The faith of Rahab demonstrated that not all Canaanites are _____.

ACTIVITY 3: *Ammonites and Moabites (A Reading)*

1. Read Deuteronomy 23:3–8. The exclusion of Ammonites and Moabites to the _____ generation is the equivalent of "never." The inclusion of Egyptians and Edomites in the _____ generation offers opportunity to demonstrate that the assimilation into the assembly of Yahweh is genuine by raising their children according to the _____.

2. Lamentations 1:10 presents Lady Jerusalem as Yahweh's wife and her holy place as the exclusive right of her husband. What act by the Neo-Babylonians does the poetic imagery refer to?
   a) murder
   b) vandalism
   c) gang rape
   d) extortion

---

* Also compare Exod 23:23–33 for the same results.

3. Isaiah 52:1 comforts Lady Jerusalem, who will no longer be violated by the _____ and _____.

4. In the texts below <u>underline</u> the verbal parallels between Deuteronomy 23:3; Lamentations 1:10; and Isaiah 52:1.

5. Use <u>broken underlining</u> to mark the terms used in Lamentations 1:10 and Isaiah 52:1 that serve as interpretive equivalents to "Ammonites and Moabites" in Deuteronomy23:3.

> An Ammonite or Moabite shall not enter the assembly of Yahweh, even to the tenth generation they shall not enter into the assembly of Yahweh, forever. (Deut 23:3 lit.)

> The enemy laid hands on all her treasures. She saw nations enter her holy place—those you have commanded, they shall not enter your assembly. (Lam 1:10 lit.)

> Awake, awake, Zion, clothe yourself with strength! Put on your garments of splendor, Jerusalem, the holy city. The uncircumcised and defiled shall not enter you again. (Isa 52:1 lit.)

6. Based on the use of Deuteronomy 23:3 in Lamentations 1:10 and in Isaiah 52:1, the terms "Ammonite and Moabite" in the law of the assembly are understood (choose one) ethnically or symbolically.

7. Read Nehemiah 13:23–26. The problem with the children of apostasy marriages speaking languages of their other parent and not the language of their Judean parent demonstrates that they (choose one) did not or did raise them according to the covenantal standards of Israel's God.

8. As noted above, in Romans 9:6 Paul says, "not all who are descended from Israel are _____." The faith of Ruth demonstrates that not all Moabites are _____.

ACTIVITY 4: *Deuteronomy and the Prophets (selected Scriptures)*

- Read the selections from Deuteronomy in the left-hand column of the chart below.
- Fill in the middle "prophet" column with the following references: • Jeremiah 3:1; • Jeremiah 13:11 (use KJV, ESV, NRSVue, at BibleGateway.com if needed); • Jeremiah 31:29–30; • Hosea 13:6; • Amos 4:4; • Amos 5:10–12; • Malachi 1:8, 13.
- Fill in the blanks of the right-hand "message" column with the following messages: • defective sacrifices; • divorce and remarriage defile; • each one judged for their own crimes; • satisfied–proud–forget Yahweh; • taunt of sacrifices every three days.

Deuteronomy	Prophet	Message
1. 8:12–14		
2. 14:28; 26:12		
3. 15:21		
4. 16:18–19		despising justice
5. 24:1–4		
6. 24:16		
7. 26:19		satire of people as Yahweh's worthless loincloth of "renown (fame)," "praise," and "honor"

8. In one sentence describe how the prophets tend to use the legal standards of Deuteronomy against their constituents in the examples above.

ACTIVITY 5: *Making It Our Own (Another Look)*

1. Read Psalm 44:17–22. Faithful people of God (choose one) suffer or never suffer. How do the claims of the psalmists help readers avoid being too mechanistic in thinking about cause-and-effect relationships between obedience and blessing versus disobedience and judgment (be sure to think collectively not only individualistically)?

2. Read Matthew 1:1–5. What are the names of the women of the nations of Canaan and of Moab listed as matriarchs of King David and the Messiah?

3. What are the implications of Matthew including these matriarchs of Messiah?

28 A VIEW OF THE OTHER SIDE
(Deuteronomy 29–34)

ACTIVITY 1: *Understanding the Chapter (A Reading)*

1. The end of Deuteronomy offers what view to readers?

    a) broken dreams

    b) the next beginning

    c) the end

    d) anticipated obedience

2. The new covenant of Deuteronomy 29 compares the expected rebellion and judgment of Israel to _____ and _____.

3. The turning point for Israel in exile is when Yahweh _____ their hearts so that they will love God and _____. Jeremiah's revelatory advances of the new covenant include putting _____ in their minds and writing it in their _____. Moses and Jeremiah speak of God doing a work in the hearts of his people to change who they are.

4. The new covenant intentionally reaches into what time?

    a) when the people will be in exile

    b) when the people will be resting in the land

    c) when the people will be worshiping at the temple

    d) when the people will be engaged in warfare

5. What points toward the present force of the new covenant teaching within Deuteronomy?

    a) presence of God's glory in the tabernacle

    b) presence of the people in the land

    c) presence of the word in the mouth and in the heart

    d) presence of the tablets of the covenant within the ark

6. Who or what was to replace Moses after his death?

    a) the ark and the tabernacle

    b) the Torah scroll and the ark of the covenant

    c) Joshua and Caleb

    d) Joshua and the Torah scroll

7. What was the function of the Torah for sinners?

    a) to act as a comfort to their despair

    b) to act as a witness against them

    c) to act as a refuge from danger

    d) to act as poison to swallow

8. What two related objects are guarded by the cherubim?

    a) the tree of life and Torah

    b) the tree of life and the body of Moses

    c) Mount Sinai and Mount Zion

    d) garden of Eden and the body of Moses

9. Deuteronomy closes with an expectation for whom?

    a) lion of Judah

    b) star out of Jacob

    c) return of Enoch

    d) prophet like Moses

10. The Torah and the gospel are not two different things. The Torah story is the _____ of the gospel story.

ACTIVITY 2: *Deuteronomy and the Prophets (selected Scriptures)*

- Read the selections from Deuteronomy in the left-hand column of the chart below.
- Fill in the middle "prophet" column with the following references: • Isaiah 1:2; • Isaiah 6:9–10; • Jeremiah 23:14; • Jeremiah 31:31–34; • Ezekiel 16:43–58; • Hosea 11:8; • Malachi 2:6.
- Fill in the blanks of the right-hand "message" column with the following messages: • another covenant; • instructions from Levi; • like Admah and Zeboyim; • listen! heavens and earth; • obstructing eyes and ears; • worse than sister Sodom.

Deuteronomy	Prophet	Message
1. 29:1		
2. 29:2–4		
3. 29:23		warm reception of false prophets in Jerusalem like Sodom and Gomorrah

Deuteronomy	Prophet	Message
4. 29:23	Ezekiel 16:43–58	
5. 29:23		
6. 32:1		
7. 33:10		

8. In one sentence describe how the prophets tend to use the expectations of Deuteronomy in their prophetic messages.

ACTIVITY 3: *Moses Sees but Does Not Cross Over (Deuteronomy 34)*

For help with geography activities, the best option is a biblical atlas from a library. In addition, many Bibles have maps near the back, or you can use the maps in *Torah Story*.

1. List the following places on the appropriate lines next to the dots that mark their locations: Jericho; Mount Nebo; plains of Moab; Zoar.

2. List the following regions on the angled dotted lines that mark their locations: Gilead; the Negev.

3. Label the following body of water: Mediterranean Sea. (There is no line.)

4. Read Deuteronomy 34:1–4. Using the names of the tribes listed in these verses, place them on the angled appropriate blank lines to mark their respective territories. Remember, one tribe needs to be placed on two lines since their region is split in half.

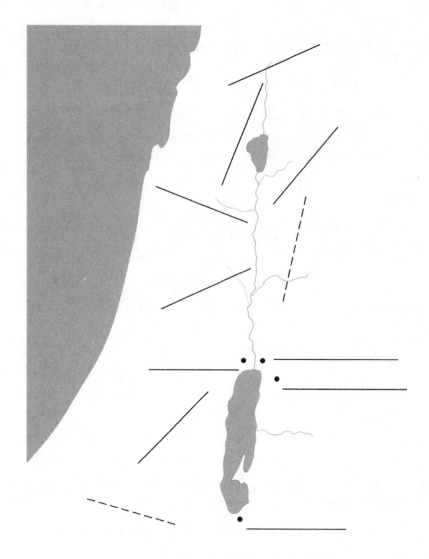

ACTIVITY 4: *Making It Our Own (A Reading)*

1. Use <u>broken underlining</u> to mark parallel language in Exodus 20:19 and Deuteronomy 5:25, 27–28.

2. Use <u>wavy underlining</u> to mark parallel language in Deuteronomy 5:25, 27–28 and 18:15–18.

> [The people] said to Moses, "You tell us and we will listen. But do not have God speak to us or we will die." (Exod 20:19 lit.)

> [25][The people said] "But now, why should we die? This great fire will consume us, and [we will die] if we hear the voice of Yahweh our God any longer. . . . [27]Go near and listen to all that Yahweh our God says. Then you tell us whatever Yahweh our God tells you. We will listen and obey." [28]Yahweh heard you when you spoke to me, and Yahweh said to me, "I have heard what this people said to you. What they said was good." (Deut 5:25, 27–28 lit.)

¹⁵[Moses said,] Yahweh your God will raise up for you a prophet like me from among you, from your fellows. You must listen to him. ¹⁶ For this is what you asked of Yahweh your God at Horeb on the day of the assembly when you said, "Let me not hear the voice of Yahweh my God nor see this great fire anymore, or I [will die]." ¹⁷ Yahweh said to me: "All that they say is good. ¹⁸ I will raise up for them a prophet like you from among their fellows, and I will put my words in his mouth. He will tell them everything I command him." (18:15–18 lit.)

3. Study the passages marked above in Exodus 20; Deuteronomy 5; and 18. What does the establishment of the institution of a prophet like Moses starting with a request of the people tell us about the dynamics of Yahweh's covenantal relationship with his people?

4. Use broken underlining to mark parallel language in Exodus 33:11 and Deuteronomy 34:10–12.

5. Use wavy underlining to mark parallel language in Deuteronomy 4:34 and 34:10–12.

6. Underline parallel language in Deuteronomy 18:15 and 34:10–12.

Yahweh would speak to Moses face to face, as one speaks to a friend. (Exod 33:11a)

Has any god ever tried to take for himself one nation out of another nation, by testings, by signs and wonders, by war, by a mighty hand and an outstretched arm, or by awesome deeds, like all the things Yahweh your God did for you in Egypt before your very eyes? (Deut 4:34 lit.)

Yahweh your God will raise up for you a prophet like me from among you, from your fellow Israelites. You must listen to him. (Deut 18:15)

¹⁰Since then, no prophet has risen in Israel like Moses, whom Yahweh knew face to face, ¹¹who did all those signs and wonders Yahweh sent him to do in Egypt—to pharaoh and to all his officials and to his whole land. ¹²For no one has ever shown the mighty hand or performed the awesome deeds that Moses did before the eyes of all Israel. (Deut 34:10–12 lit.)

7. What two characteristics of Moses become expectations for a coming prophet like Moses in Deuteronomy 34:10–12?

8. What aspect of the expectation does Peter focus on when he identifies Messiah as the prophet like Moses in Acts 3:22–23? How do followers of the Messiah need to respond to his instruction?

29 REINTRODUCING THE TORAH

Paul Venning

ACTIVITY 1: *Understanding the Chapter (A Reading)*

1. Put the following elements in the correct sequence relative to the storyline of the Torah by numbering them 1 to 9:

_____ expectation of the Judah-king to rule the nations in the last days

_____ holiness of Yahweh dwells with his people in the tabernacle

_____ rebellion in the garden

_____ redemption from Egyptian bondage

_____ new beginning after the flood

_____ explanation and teaching by Moses on the plains of Moab

_____ call of Abraham

_____ revelation at the mountains

_____ the older generation falls into temptation in the wilderness

Matching

2. ____ This book is Genesis-shaped by extending the sacred space of the tabernacle to demonstrate the holiness of the Creator.

3. ____ This book is Genesis-shaped by offering a new beginning and setting before the people a choice for life and death as in the garden.

4. ____ This book is Genesis-shaped because it narrates the creation of the nation of Israel.

5. ____ This book is Genesis-shaped by depicting the interrelationship of the tribes of Israel and the nation's place among the nations according to patterns established in the narrative of the Hebrew ancestors.

A Exodus

B Leviticus

C Numbers

D Deuteronomy

6. The _____ _____ refers to Torah and the Deuteronomistic Narrative (Joshua, Judges, Samuel, _____) as a unified serial narrative going from the creation of the heavens and earth to the fall of _____.

7. The story of rebellion in the _____ prefigures the Primary Narrative when the rebels are exiled to the _____.

8. The basic pattern of _____–_____–_____ sets the Latter Prophets and Writings into a theological conversation with the Primary Narrative. This shared pattern is all about the meaning of these things in the light of the _____.

9. The Torah's story establishes and the rest of the Hebrew Scriptures interact with the question: How will the _____ of God prevail over the _____ revolution? The _____ _____ provides the answer to the question.

10. The _____ _____ is not opposed to the gospel nor is it the gospel. The Torah story is the _____ of the gospel. The story that begins in _____ reaches its height on the Skull.

ACTIVITY 2: *Making It Our Own (Another Look)*

1. Study Deuteronomy 31:24–29 and 1 Timothy 1:8–11. In what way do Moses and Paul agree on the function of the Torah?

2. Study John 5:39–47. What are two of the key ways that Moses speaks of the expected Messiah in the Torah?

CREDITS

The vast majority of the activities in the *Workbook* are based directly on *Torah Story*. For indebtedness see citations therein.

The logic of Chapter 4, activity 4—the tenfold use of "according to their kinds" versus "in the image of God"—is indebted to observations in Ellen van Wolde, "The Text as Eloquent Guide: Rhetorical, Linguistic, and Literary Features in Genesis 1," in *Literary Structure and Rhetorical Strategies in the Hebrew Bible*, ed. L. J. de Regt, J. de Waard, and J. Fokkelman (Winona Lake, IN: Eisenbrauns, 1996), 134–51.

The basic elements of Chapter 7, activity 4 related to the growing of the Abrahamic promise in Genesis is based on Gary Edward Schnittjer, *Old Testament Use of Old Testament* (Grand Rapids: Zondervan Academic, 2021), 12 (Table G1).

The topographical images of Chapter 7, activity 5 are from public domain, namely, Jesse L. Hurlbut, *Bible Atlas: A Manual of Biblical Geography and History*, rev. ed. (Chicago: Rand McNally & Company, 1910), 31. The modifications to these images: Copyright © 2023 Gary Edward Schnittjer. All rights reserved.

Elements in Chapter 10, activity 5 regarding the advancement of the expectations of the blessing of Judah in Scripture are based on Gary Edward Schnittjer, "Blessing of Judah as Generative Expectation," *Bibliotheca Sacra* 177 (2020): 21–22. The translations of Genesis 49:11 and Zechariah 9:9 are based in part on Kenneth C. Way, "Donkey Domain: Zechariah 9:9 and Lexical Semantics," *Journal of Biblical Literature* 129.1 (2010): 105–14.

Number 4 in Chapter 13, activity 4 is indebted to Gary N. Knoppers, "The Relationship of the Priestly Genealogies to the History of the High Priesthood in Jerusalem," in *Judah and the Judeans in the Neo-Babylonian Period*, ed. Oded Lipschitz and Joseph Blenkinsopp (Winona Lake, IN: Eisenbrauns, 2003), 124.

Elements in Chapter 14, activity 3 are based in large part on Carmen Joy Imes, *Bearing God's Name: Why Sinai Still Matters* (Downers Grove, IL: IVP Academic, 2019), 48–51; idem, *Bearing YHWH's Name at Sinai: A Reexamination of the Name Command of the Decalogue* (University Park, PA: Eisenbrauns, 2018), 113–39; idem, "Metaphor at Sinai: Cognitive Linguistics in the Decalogue and Covenant Code," *Bulletin for Biblical Research* 29.3 (2019): 358.

Elements in Chapter 14, activity 4 are indebted to Moshe Greenberg, "Some Postulates of Biblical Criminal Law," in Moshe Greenberg, *Studies in the Bible and Jewish Thought* (Philadelphia: Jewish Publication Society, 1995), 25–41; Christine Hayes, "Lecture 10. Biblical Law: The Three Legal Corpora of JE (Exodus), P (Leviticus and Numbers) and D," Introduction to the Old Testament (RLST 145) (class lecture, Yale University, New Haven, CT, December 6, 2012), available online at https://youtu.be/iJ5qYM24vUA (25:39), accessed March 1, 2015; idem, *Introduction to Bible* (New Haven: Yale University Press, 2012), 135–46, esp. 145–46; idem, *What's Divine about Divine Law? Early Perspectives* (Princeton: Princeton University Press, 2015), 21; Joseph Ryan Kelly, "The Ethics of Inclusion: The גר and the אזרח in the Passover to Yhwh," *Bulletin of Biblical Research* 23.2 (2013): 155–66.

Figure of tabernacle in Chapter 15, activity 2 created by Gary Edward Schnittjer is based on a diagram in Everett Fox, *The Five Books of Moses* (New York: Schocken Books, 1995), 491.

Elements in Chapter 15, activity 4 are based on Schnittjer, *OT Use of OT*, 24–26.

Elements in Chapter 20, activity 2 are based on Gary Edward Schnittjer, *Torah Story Video Lectures* (Grand Rapids: Zondervan Academic, 2017), Chapter 20, part 1.

Elements in Chapter 22, activity 3 are based on Gary Edward Schnittjer, "Kadesh Infidelity of Deuteronomy 1 and Its Synoptic Implications," *Journal of the Evangelical Theological Society* 63.1 (2020): 116–17; idem, *OT Use of OT*, 517–18.

Elements in Chapter 23, activity 2 are indebted to Schnittjer, "Blessing of Judah," 22–24; idem, *OT Use of OT*, 293–95.

Elements in Chapter 25, activity 2 are indebted to Schnittjer, "Kadesh Infidelity," esp. 108–9, and elements in Chapter 25, activity 4 indebted to Schnittjer, *OT Use of OT*, 97–100.

Elements in Chapter 27, activity 3 are indebted to Schnittjer, *OT Use of OT*, 238–41, 606–7.

Elements in Chapter, 28, activity 4 are indebted to Schnittjer, *OT Use of OT*, 130–31, 146–48.

ACKNOWLEDGMENTS

Many activities in this workbook come from classroom workshop sessions in courses and electives on the Torah over the past three decades. Thank you to my students for spirited discussion and debate. It is a pleasure to study and to wrestle together with Torah's call to God's redemptive will.

I am grateful for the work of several teaching assistants and research assistants who helped with ideas for this *Workbook*. Thank you to Briana Borowski, Courtney Bottge, Katie Colabella, Bobby Larew, and Cai Matthews. In some cases, the research assistants designed an initial working draft of activities included herein based on *Torah Story* and its associated videos and/or my lecture notes, classroom visuals, and other teaching materials. Although many of their ideas were not used, they sometimes sparked ideas for other activities that have been included herein. I also offer my gratitude to Caroline Master, Hannah Conger, and Rachel Hevalow for checking (and re-checking more than once) the answer key for professors against the textbook and making associated notations. I greatly appreciate the generous support of Cairn University and its Divinity School for funding teaching and research assistants.

I offer my gratitude to the students who worked through an early draft of the activities in this *Workbook* and offered critical feedback and suggestions. Thank you to the students in my Pentateuch sections at Cairn University spring 2020. Thank you to Carmen Joy Imes and her Torah students in spring 2020. And after the activities were adjusted based on the early feedback, thanks go to my Pentateuch students over the last several semesters for additional evaluation and suggestions.

Special thanks go to Barbara Arnold for looking up every verse reference in this *Workbook* to check for errors. Barbara also offered feedback on grammar and other suggestions for improvement of activities. Thank you to the blind academic proofreader for helpful feedback. Thank you to the team at Zondervan Academic. I am grateful to Nancy Erickson for several observations, suggestions, as well as keeping this project on track. I offer my appreciation to Kait Lamphere for interior design.

Thank you to my wife Cheri for proofreading a draft of the *Workbook*.

Any mistakes that remain are my responsibility.